a

different

kind of

same

a

different

kind of

same

a memoir
kelley clink

SHE WRITES PRESS

Published 2015
Printed in the United States of America
ISBN: 978-1-63152-999-3
Library of Congress Control Number: 2014952583

For information, address:
She Writes Press
1563 Solano Ave #546
Berkeley, CA 94707

She Writes Press is a division of Spark Point Studio, LLC.

"Flame Thrower Love," by Dead Boys. 1978. Album: *We Have Come For Your Children*. Writers: Stiv Bators, Jimmy Zero, William James Wilden. Copyright: Larry Spier Music LLC O.B.O. Cbgb Music Inc., Dead Boys Music, Omfug Music, WB Music Corp.

"It's Not Enough," by Johnny Thunders & The Heartbreakers. 1977. Album: *L.A.M.F.* Writer: John Genzale. Copyright: EMI Music Publishing.

"Sloop John B." by The Beach Boys. 1966. Alubm: *Pet Sounds*. Writers: Songwriters: Don Wilson, Bob Bogle, Nole Edwards, Melvin Taylor. Copyright: EMI Music Publishing

Parts of this book were originally printed, in slightly different form, in the following publications:

"Siblings" Under the Sun, Summer 2008
"Self-Portraits" The Gettysburg Review, Fall 2009
"Valentine to a Midwestern Childhood" The Prose-Poem Project, Winter 2010
"Peace, Redefined" Shambhala Sun, July 2012
"Surfacing" Colorado Review, Summer 2013

For Matt

contents

surfacing

prologue: siblings

I don't actually remember the day my parents brought my brother home from the hospital, but over the years I've invented a memory. It plays in my mind like a sepia-toned Super 8 home movie, old photographs and stories brought to life. A flash of light like the glare of an empty projector on a white dining room wall, and I appear: three years old, sitting on a worn yellow couch in a pink nightgown and fuzzy pink slippers. I wave and pull the corners of my mouth into a forced-looking, rectangular smile. It is the smile that appears in all the pictures taken of me around this time, the smile of someone trying to be a big girl, a good girl. The smile of someone who senses excitement in the air but doesn't understand it. The tense, pained smile of a new big sister.

There are my parents, standing in the doorway of the living room. Dad is tall and stick thin, with shadows under his eyes, a thick brown mustache barely disguising his youth. He wears a charcoal-colored satin jacket and holds a blue suitcase. Mom's light brown hair is permed and a baggy T-shirt covers the thighs of her bell-bottom jeans. In her arms is a small rolled blanket with a piggy face peeking out of it, eyes closed. My parents grin. Dad puts down the suitcase and the two of them walk over to the couch, settle on either side of me. Mom switches the bundle from her right arm to her left so that I can get a better look. I touch my brother's tiny hand. It moves slightly, but the rest of him is still. I touch the fuzz on top of his head. This time he awakens and begins to cry. Mom switches him back to her right arm and rocks him gently as she gets up from the sofa and leaves the frame. Dad follows. I look after them and begin to cry as well. I get up from the sofa, walk toward the camera, and then there is darkness.

For the next eight years, those preadolescent years where hair length and color-coded clothing are the main ways to differentiate boys and girls, my brother and I look the same. Small rounded noses, wide-set eyebrows, soft jawlines, and blunt chins. Short, bony legs and arms. Xylophone rib cages. Our faces the perfect blend of our parents, we seem to belong to no one but each other. Even after puberty frizzes my hair and squares his jaw, we still look more like each other than like anyone else in the family. And yet we are completely opposite: my hair brown and his blond; my eyes dark enough at times to be indistinguishable from my pupils, his bright and shifting from blue to green to gray. But our expressions, our voices, our mannerisms, the jokes we make, the stories we love, the people and places we know, are the same. Our faces are the same. It's easy to forget that we aren't, so I do.

beginnings

unsaid

M_y brother and I spoke for the last time on the afternoon of April 26, 2004—a Monday. Home from work with a sprained ankle, I decided to call him because I was bored. Because I figured that, since he was still in college, there was a good chance he'd be home in the middle of the day. Because I'd been trying to make more of an effort to talk to him. In the four years since Matt had left Alabama, left home, to go to Rutgers, since I'd gotten married and moved to Chicago, finished graduate school and started working at DePaul University's library, we'd grown apart. I was ready for us to grow back together. My efforts usually ended up as messages on his answering machine that were sometimes returned with short phone calls, sometimes with emails. I respected that. I knew that breaking away from the family was a necessary stage in our development as individuals. Matt was three years younger and had more individualizing to do. I could wait. But I wanted him to know I was there when he was ready.

In bed with the cordless phone, my ankle propped up on a stack of pillows, I turned to the S page of my address book—a reminder that I hadn't been trying hard enough. He'd had that phone number for almost two years, and I still didn't know it by heart.

"Hello?" he said.

"Hey! It's me. What's up?"

"Not much. What's up with you?"

"I'm just sitting in bed. I sprained my ankle this weekend at our soccer game."

"Well, that's what you get for playing sports. That's why I sit on my ass and do nothing."

"Yeah, whatever. How was the cancer fundraising dance-a-thon?"

"Grueling, actually. They literally would not let us stop dancing except to go to the bathroom. We were on our feet for twenty-four hours."

"What? That's crazy! I thought this was supposed to be a fun thing."

"Yeah, so did I. I'm sending out thank-yous this week, by the way, so keep an eye on the mail."

"Okay."

Pause.

"So . . . did work give you time off or something?" he asked.

"Yeah. It's kind of pointless for me to go in, seeing as I can't even walk and half my job is shelving big-ass boxes in the archives. I've been reading one of the Faulkner books you gave me," I said.

"Oh yeah? How is it?"

"It's really good, actually. But other than that, I'm pretty bored."

Pause.

"Maybe you should learn to play the bagpipes," he said.

"What?" I laughed.

"Yeah, I have a friend who is. You learn them one pipe at a time, so he's just got this clarinet-looking thing, no bag. He's pretty terrible."

I laughed again. "Okay, I don't know about that. I've only got a week, you know."

"Yeah."

Longer pause.

"Well, I better get going."

I don't remember who said that last part, he or I, but I remember what came next. Another pause, this one expanding exponentially, where a single thought surged: *Tell him you love him.* Three words, small but dense, heavy on the back of my tongue. Too heavy to move, and before I could try he filled the void with the midwestern masculine alternative:

"Take care."

And I said, "You too."

I think about it still, how you never know which two seconds will weigh on your heart for a lifetime. In my mind I am allowed to go back, allowed to change one thing—just three words. Sometimes I say, "I love you."

And sometimes I say, "Don't do it."

<hr/>

May 1, 2004. A Saturday. My parents were out of milk and eggs that morning, so Mom went to the grocery store. The police came, and left, while she was gone. When she returned, Dad was standing at the kitchen counter. By the look on his face, she told me later, she knew that someone had died. She asked who it was, and he didn't answer. She asked again. Was it her father? No. Her son.

I imagine she felt the same thing I did a few minutes later, when they called me with the news—a stomach rush, fast and cold, like I was trapped on an elevator and the cable had snapped.

The phone rang around 10:00 a.m. I was still in bed, tucked under a leaden cloud of painkillers because the crutches for my sprained ankle had pinched a nerve in my neck. My husband's voice was a low rumble in the hallway after the second ring, and I had started to let myself sink back under when Ryan opened the door, strode across the room, and shoved a handset in my face. He held the other cordless phone against his ear.

"It's your dad. He says he needs to talk to us."

I pushed myself into a sitting position, and the blood drained from my head in a shower of tiny stars.

"Hello?"

"It's your brother. . . ." I heard the thinness in my father's voice, brittle, cracking, but there weren't enough seconds for me to decipher the register of disaster. I didn't have time to wonder why he needed us both to listen.

"He . . . he passed away."

Passed away. A layer to soften the blow. Easier to speak, easier to hear. The double *s* a hushing sound, like the starched slip of a sheet pulled over a corpse to hide his face. A sheet I had to pull back to uncover the short, hard truth. Died.

Dead.

I began to cry—tears that I'd questioned for nearly a decade, lying awake in bed at night, the cocoon of blankets around my body as snug as the pocket of numbness around my heart, wondering if years of Paxil and Lexapro had killed my soul.

Passed away. As if it had been slow, as if Matt's soul had eased out of the world on a gentle gust of wind. As if he'd been fighting a wasting disease for months, years. Of course he had been. He was diagnosed with bipolar disorder at the age of fifteen, two years after I'd been diagnosed with depression. And even though in that moment I conjured a list of sudden deaths—a car crash, a mugging, a fight, an aneurism—I said, "He killed himself, didn't he?"

And my father said, "Yes."

I asked him how, and he told me. Hanging.

I don't know what I thought next. Maybe nothing. When I resurrect the memory now, my inner monologue is silent. Even the sound of my crying has faded. But I know I was still crying, because I remember the feel of it, like gravel rolling in my chest.

Then my father said, "Listen, your mom is going to call you back on the cell phone. I have to call more people. She's going to call you right now, okay?" And, "I love you."

Not the first time he'd ever said those words to me, but for some reason the first time I can remember them.

And then everything was warm and dark. The gravel in my chest had a rhythm and it was soothing. There were still no thoughts—only two bodies on a bed, Ryan's holding mine. Time didn't exist until I realized how much of it had passed. Thirty minutes. Too much. Panic froze my tears.

"Oh my God, why hasn't my mom called? Dad said she was going to call right away. What's going on?" I pulled out the phone, buried under the covers, pressed the green button, and held it to my ear.

"There's no dial tone. What the hell is going on?"

Ryan's mouth dropped open. "I left the other phone off the hook when I grabbed the cordless. . . ."

"You mean she's been trying to call me this whole time and getting a busy signal?"

I felt sick.

Ryan jumped out of bed, thundered down the stairs, and the phone in my hand rang to life.

The memory stops there. I have no recollection of my mother's voice, her first words to me or mine to her. I remember only one part of that phone call, a blip somewhere in the middle, when I recalled in a flash that I still hadn't received the card my brother had told me he was sending on Monday. I set the phone down, hobbled out the front door without my crutches, down the steps into the foyer, and jerked open our mailbox.

It was there. Right on top. A small, white envelope, my name and address in that crooked handwriting that seemed to have arrested in the fourth grade, much like our father's. The envelope had a Valentine's Day stamp, candy hearts, inked over with the *Shrek* promo that the post office was using at the time: GREETINGS FROM FAR FAR AWAY.

I tore into it, expecting some kind of explanation. An apology. A goodbye. A mistake. I scanned the note written inside: brief pleasantries, an update on his job search, thoughts about what he was reading and writing for school.

I limped back into the apartment and picked up the phone. "It came."

"Well," my mother asked, "what does it say?"

I shook my head. "Nothing."

their genes

Two years before he died, my brother started a blog. He didn't tell us about it, but Mom found it anyway. A student who worked for her at the University of Alabama library was a member of the same blogging community, and she'd friended Matt and told Mom about his page. Mom then told me. After reading the blog, I sent my brother an email commenting on a porn clip he'd recently posted, as well as his hair, which he'd dyed black:

> *I suppose it's time I stopped thinking of you as my little brother and started thinking of you as a sexually frustrated onanist with a bad dye job. Anyway, this looks cool but it says I have to pay to join unless an existing member invites me. You want to invite me?*

He replied:

> *I'd invite you but I already used all my codes. Where'd you hear about my blog, anyways? I hope mom and dad haven't been reading it; I know they are aware of it, so I guess it's safe to say that mom has made an effort. Whatever, I'm demented, it's their genes.*

Their genes. By then the irony of this statement was a fact of our lives. While mental illness and suicides often trickle through generations, handed down like tarnished heirlooms, it seemed our family was the exception. No suicides or hospitalizations, no addictions or abuse. In fact, our parents were the two most normal people I'd ever seen, so normal it was abnormal. They were like the Cleavers, our friends often said. Dad worked nine to five, coached T-ball, and barbecued on the weekends. Mom stayed home with us, volunteered at school, made our lunches, and folded our laundry. They yelled at each other a handful of times, yelled at us a handful more, but they didn't drink or smoke or do drugs, didn't hit us or each other, didn't break things or cry uncontrollably. They made life look easy, which might be why Matt and I were so confused when we found out it wasn't.

As my brother and I took turns falling apart, cycling through therapists, psychiatrists, and medications, I felt sorry for them. What could they possibly have done to deserve us? In the brief slices of time when things were okay, I teased them. Karma for some past life offenses, I said. And in the larger slices of time when things weren't okay, it was part of the unspoken bond Matt and I shared. Their genes. We were the only two people in the world made up of those two people, and yet we'd inherited none of their stability.

It is the end of August 2012, and outside my office window the leaves of a honey locust shrivel in the heat. I pick up the phone and call my father. I want to talk about the past. I want to understand the veneer, the pageant, of my childhood. Of course I don't say that. I don't know how to say that without sounding accusatory and melodramatic. Instead, I tell him that I'm exploring the roots of mental illness in the family—rather, the apparent lack of them.

"Things were different back then," my dad says. "Nobody talked about that kind of stuff. You had to be going through psychosis to end up medicated or in a hospital. Withdrawing, sitting alone in your room all the time, those weren't signs of depression. That was just how someone was.

"Hell," he says, "if you transplanted everyone to the present, there'd be all kinds of diagnoses."

His father, he says, had a "dark side" and became increasingly depressed toward the end of his life. One of his sisters went through years of therapy. He had an uncle, a World War II vet, who died by suicide. He doesn't know any details. This is the first I've heard of any of this.

But what about you, I want to ask. *What did you inherit? What did you pass down to us—aside from silence?*

But I don't. Because even though we've come a long way, that silence is buried deep in our code. You could call it midwestern stoicism or good old-fashioned politeness. I've come to think of it as a survival skill, albeit a rusty and antique one—it still works, kind of, but it's a little dangerous and awkward to use. Life is hard; we aren't born knowing how to deal with it. Some people in the past, like Buddha, have suggested sitting, breathing, and observing our feelings. Others, like Jesus, have suggested we open up our hearts and lean on each other. And then others—my ancestors, and probably yours—decided that it was a hell of a lot easier to bottle up their feelings, quit thinking so much, accept the information people offered, and then mind their own goddamn business.

This silent, MYOB gene is present on both sides of the family. Turns out, however, that once my mom and I got started talking about serious shit a few years after Matt died, we couldn't stop.

It was strange at first. Really strange. My mother had been a Saint throughout my childhood: a devout Catholic whose well of self-sacrifice never ran dry. She didn't get angry, or petty, or bored. She was never jealous or selfish or lazy. She was a pinnacle of motherhood, womanhood, *human*hood, that was impossible to live up to.

"It was an act," she says now. "I just wanted people to like me. I felt so unloved as a kid. I got the most praise when I followed the rules perfectly and did things for other people." She wanted childhood to be different for my brother and me: she wanted us to feel loved unconditionally. "There is nothing—*nothing*—you can do," she used to say, "that will make me stop loving you." I can't speak for Matt, but that concept frightened me. I think it was because I didn't believe her. She was a perfect mother—and I wasn't a perfect kid. I lashed out when I didn't get my way. I half-assed my chores. I was too skinny and I had buckteeth. I didn't get the best grades in the class and I hated going to church. I was bossy and whiny and I didn't like to share. My head was constantly full of mean thoughts, fears, and strange desires. How could she—how could anyone—love me?

Back then I thought that love was a warm, fuzzy, Christmas-morning kind of glow—one it was safe to assume my mother felt all the time. I didn't know you could love someone and still occasionally want to punch him in the face. That you could love someone and not want to see her, say, more than once a year. That you could love someone even if he voted for "the other guy." And my mother wasn't the one who finally taught me these things. I learned them slowly, over a couple of miserable, self-deprecating decades. Mostly from the Twelve Steps, the Dalai Lama, Thich Nhat Hanh, and Anne Lamott.

I was angry with my mother for a while after she started opening up to me. Why hadn't she told me any of this before? Why had she let me grow up feeling so broken and alone? And what if Matt had known this? Would it have made a difference?

Then I realized some things. For instance, that she felt broken and alone as a child, and so she was trying to be the antithesis of her parents. That if she'd expressed all of her feelings all of the time, I might have grown up a lot more anxious and depressed than I did. And that she *had* told me some things about herself and her past when I was an adolescent. But I didn't hear her stories about how she channeled all of her fear and control issues into exercise and anorexia. I didn't see anything odd about her father's tendency to avoid leaving the house for years at a time, to sleep all day and sit at the kitchen table all night, smoking unfiltered Pall Malls, washing his Valium down with sweet iced tea.

The Buddhist monk Yongey Mingyur Rinpoche says that to combat basic unease, "we tend to invest the 'inhabitants' of our relative or conditional world . . . with qualities that enhance their semblance of solidness and stability."

My mother adds, "You can't see these things as a child. Not until you've lived through enough yourself to understand them. That's when you have compassion."

———

After I emailed Matt about his blog, he asked Mom to stop reading it. I felt bad, but I wasn't sure if it was because I'd ratted her out or because I'd infiltrated his private life. And, even though I hadn't been directed to, I stopped reading his blog, too.

I told myself it was because I wanted to respect his privacy. I hadn't lived through enough to know about the MYOB gene yet. I didn't know that I'd been conditioned to assume, to build out the unknown details of people's lives in my head, to finish the picture on my own. I'd become immune to omission. I'd stopped needing to know the truth.

I didn't visit Matt's blog again until the day I learned about his death. When I attempted to access the page, I found a bright pink screen with a single posting:

I have made an oath to suspend making new friends for an undetermined amount of time. As such, my journal is "friends only." Fuck off unless you were my friend prior to 4/1/[0]4.

I stared at that screen for hours, wondering about the words locked behind it. I wondered whether our suffering was as inescapable and indelible as our fingerprints. I wondered whether their genes had killed him. And, if they had, whether they'd kill me, too.

us

Even though my brother died in New Jersey, even though he and I had lived in Tuscaloosa, Alabama, for six years and our parents still lived there at the time of his death, there was never a question asked, never a decision to be made—he would be buried in Michigan. The day before his wake, my parents, my husband, and I went to the cemetery in suburban Detroit where my father's parents are buried. As we sat in the office, discussing burial options, we made a quick decision: we bought five plots—one for each of us. It made sense at the time. The future we'd expected had been erased, replaced with a dark gray fog of uncertainty, and we clung to the few things we could control. We would all be buried in Michigan. The origin of memories, our first understanding of home.

From the time my memory kicked in until the time I was six years old, my family lived on the lower level of a two-flat in southwestern Detroit. It had light blue siding with white trim and a concrete slab of front porch with a black iron railing. There was a thick, beveled mirror on the door of the hall closet, claw feet on the bathtub, and peeling gray stairs beyond the kitchen that led down to the basement or up to the neighbor's apartment. The sunny yellow light of the kitchen was always fighting against the dark of those stairs. My parents' bedroom was at the front of the house, off the living room, and mine was next to theirs. When Matt came along, Mom and Dad converted the closet beside the bathroom into a nursery.

I remember the sound of my bare feet slapping the wood floors, the screeching tires and shouts of the neighborhood, the kids next door, my friends from preschool and kindergarten, my grandparents, aunts, uncles, and cousins. But I don't really remember my brother during those years. Even after he started to walk, talk, smile. I remember the spider-infested sandbox in the backyard, the pink and white–checkered curtains on my bedroom windows, the stuffed dog I named Peanut Butter, but not the sound of his voice feeling its way through my name, or prying blocks from his chubby fists and toy cars from his drooling mouth. Those things happened, of course. But, as is so often the case, the truth of our beginning isn't the same as the memory. For me, he never lived in that house—except for one small moment, captured in a photograph.

In the picture I wear a red, white, and blue sailor dress, thick brown bangs cut straight across at my eyebrows. Matt wears a red shirt and red shorts, his hair a blond cap of wisps. Our smiles gather our cheeks into mounds, and the photographer's flash glitters in our eyes.

I was a month shy of four years old that day, so Matt had just turned one. The photographer had come to the house to take our portrait in the living room. He unrolled his gray sheet of backdrop behind the coffee table, which is what we sat on, Matt in front of me between my legs. I was told to put my arms around him, which I did, and there it begins. *He* begins. His weight against my body, the heat of his skin against my skin, the smell of his head sweet and warm like bread dough.

When I close my eyes, I am four years old again. I feel him filling the space in front of me. The memory is as brief as the photographer's flash—say "cheese"—and my brother is gone. I am alone again.

I was alone again, back then, until we moved.

———

We left Detroit to escape our wife-beating, alcoholic next-door neighbor and the junkie thief who lived across the street. To find playgrounds that weren't littered with broken glass and nights that weren't punctured by the pop of gunshots or the wail of sirens. We went to the place where everyone else who could leave went: the suburbs.

For me, the childhood Matt and I shared began when we moved a dozen or so miles outside of Detroit, into the house on Haller Street in Livonia, and ended six years later when, at the age of twelve, I became all-knowing, all mature, and mortified by my family. But from the time I was six to the time I was eleven, life was about as close to perfect as it could be. Those years have merged into a mass of Popsicles and Kool-Aid, the rainbow at the edge of the sprinkler and the sticky-sweet smell of mulberries ripening in the sun; Saturday-morning cartoons and roller-skating in the basement, clouds of charcoal smoke and picnic tables piled with potato salad; Hide and Seek, Pop-Up, Rain on the Roof, and Four Square; the crunch of leaves beneath our shoes and the thunk of candy into a plastic pumpkin pail; the tangy smell of burning branches and the sparkle of a frost-sprayed lawn; turkey, stuffing, and football; snow—a shared sled on a small but thrilling slope, the morning dark and the scrape of shovels, powdered diamonds glittering under the streetlamp, red faces, wet feet, hot chocolate; tiny purple flowers beaded with ice, flares of crimson chests against a gray sky melting blue, blankets of fallen buds on the sidewalks, and the trees whispering to us again.

Of course, those years weren't perfect. There were fights with friends, fights with each other, punishments, problems at school, and dead hamsters and goldfish. But for whatever reason those memories are separate, flung far by the dervish of myth. Perhaps edited out to justify my rage after Dad got a new job and we moved to Alabama just before my sophomore year of high school—the absolute good of Michigan to balance my teenage pronouncement of the absolute evil of the South.

Whenever and why-ever it happened, it's the picture I have now. If I really try, I can isolate specific memories. Sometimes I can even reinhabit them. I can lie beneath our poplar tree on a summer afternoon and feel the grass against my skin, taste the copper of cold water from the hose, see Matt's body curled in the crook of the box elder and hear the thud of his feet when he jumps down. Other memories I can only watch, a stranger from a distant future looking in. There are too many to choose from, too few that give enough, and one that is my favorite.

Every summer during our childhood, Matt and I spent countless hours in our "clubhouses," the misnomer for the remnants of a square mile of forest once connecting our backyard to those of our neighbors. The first two years we lived in the house on Haller Street there was nothing but trees from our yard all the way to the next road, and Matt and I were explorers. We crashed through bushes and branches, waded in large, slug-filled puddles, and jabbed sticks into the holes where Mom said snakes lived. But the world was ever spreading, and most of the trees were bulldozed to build a McDonald's. An empty field remained the buffer for the small, leftover corner of woods that became our clubhouses.

We divided the area based on a path stamped into the vegetation that led to the field. On the side of the path closest to our yard was my clubhouse, a climbing tree surrounded by treasure: sticks and rocks, old bottles, and occasionally mini-golf balls that had been whacked over the fence of a now-defunct putt-putt when the field was still woods, their colors dulled by dirt and exposure. Matt's was on the other side, a bed of ivy that grew up a gentle slope, crawled onto a few pieces of rusty chain-link fence that no longer held anything in or out, and twisted up the branches of trees, twining together into a canopy.

The memory begins in the brush at the back of my neighbor's yard, facing the clubhouses. It is a warm summer day; the bright sun and knee-high dry grass that mark the entrance to the open field are a stark contrast with the clubhouses, which are cool and shaded and green, the dirt smooth from our many footsteps, the constant rustle of leaves in the breeze like waves crashing and pulling on sand.

I see Matt first, six years old, sitting in a tire dropped into the ivy. Drips of sunlight work their way through the leaves and speckle his fine blond hair, his still-round child's face, his skinny brown limbs. I don't remember when we found the tire, how it became his. I was jealous and frequently rolled it into my clubhouse to sit on, but not in this memory. In this memory the tire is his, and there I see my nine-year-old self, nestled in the gnarled tangle of roots at the base of my tree.

We sit silently together in a world of our own making, lost in thoughts I cannot know. I watch those two consciousnesses, one never having known a time before the other, neither imagining a time without.

Nothing happens. No matter how long I stay and watch, we only sit. We never speak. We don't have to. We just exist.

━━━━━━━

You can freeze a memory like that forever—but you can't freeze a moment. Things change, time marches on, nothing is permanent. In a few short years, I grew a foot. Hair sprouted beneath my arms and between my legs. A swath of pimples erupted across my forehead and chin.

At twelve years old I was (overnight, it seemed) too old to ride bikes, run through sprinklers, invent games, hunt treasure in the field, or use the clubhouses—unless it was to sneak drags off cigarette butts scavenged from the ashtrays of my friends' parents. And Matt was too young to do what I did, which was called "hanging out" and mainly involved going to the mall with my friends to shoplift lipstick and beg quarters off old people so we could buy tacos. My brother became a reminder of my hideously embarrassing years as a child. Years when I hadn't known anything about anything, when I'd been a geek, a baby who'd let adults order her around. Now that I was in middle school, practically a teenager, I was way cooler than Matt would ever be, and I made sure he knew it. At home I spent most of my time in my room with the door closed, blaring hip-hop through my headphones (cassettes with PARENTAL ADVISORY warnings that I hid in a shoebox at the back of my closet). And what I said to him, to everyone in my family, most often was, "Leave me alone."

━━━━━━━

We grew close again after my parents moved us to Alabama, and we stayed that way until I graduated high school and started college.

Friends of mine with siblings tell me that this pattern continues throughout adulthood. You come together, you grow apart, you come back together again. As with any relationship, you change at differ-ent speeds and you need space to do it. At the time of his death, I didn't quite understand this. I assumed the emotional distance that had crept between us again was a matter of waiting out our staggered formative years. I was sure that someday, when the turmoil of growing up was done, we would meet again in the garden of adulthood and everything would be like it was before.

And in a way, it is. The boundaries of age and gender that divided us during Matt's lifetime disintegrated when he died. He is with me constantly now, the way he was in the woods of our childhood—silent, but near. A presence, a memory. Lounging patiently in my periphery.

them

The funeral parlor where we held Matt's wake was about a mile and a half from our old house on Haller Street—practically next door to my grandmother's church, catty-corner from her grocery store, and half a block away from a Middle Eastern restaurant I'd hung out at with an older, cooler friend the summer before we moved. It had been there (the funeral home, not the restaurant) for over fifty years. I'd never noticed it. While we'd lived in Michigan it had been scenery, backdrop, a part of the everyday landscape of my life that, never needed, had never come into focus. And after we moved to Alabama, every part of that landscape blurred, faded. Each time we came back to visit relatives, the places we'd left behind—stores, schools, houses—that hadn't changed, that hadn't been torn down or remodeled, felt smaller and farther away. By the end of our first year in Alabama and the beginning of my depression, I knew Michigan would never be the same, never be home, again. It was relegated to memory. A beginning, and now an end.

While the bulk of people who attended Matt's wake were from Michigan (family members, old neighbors, friends, and former coworkers), there were people there from everywhere he'd lived. Jasper and Lee, two of Matt's best friends from Alabama, had come. They were boys I had known for years, who had walked up and down the hallway to and from Matt's bedroom, jammed with him on their guitars and started bands, sat around in our kitchen, petted our dog, joked with our parents. Seeing them there with my extended family, against the faded backdrop of my past, was as strange and exciting as running into a friend in a foreign airport. I wanted to laugh just as much as I wanted to cry, and I hugged them the way I wished I could hug him—tightly, as if they belonged to me. I suppose in a way they did. They were the last everyday friends of his I'd known.

Five of Matt's friends from Jersey were there, and their young, unfamiliar faces haunted the corners of the room. Two of them were from the campus at Newark, where Matt spent his first two years, and three were from the campus at New Brunswick, where he'd transferred because of the greater availability of classes in his political science major.

I had a secondhand familiarity with the kids from Newark: Oscar, Matt's roommate the year before he transferred, and Gwen, an ex-girlfriend who'd remained a close friend. I knew their stories, had seen their pictures. The other three—a guy with curly black hair and two girls (a platinum blond and a brunette)—were complete strangers, the literal embodiment of how far apart my brother and I had drifted. My mother, possibly sensing their discomfort and recognizing that they belonged to Matt alone, spoke to them first. She told me later that the brunette was a close friend from New Brunswick. I recognized her name. She was, Mom had told me months before Matt's death, someone he'd had feelings for. Someone he'd never told me about himself.

I don't know why I didn't speak to Matt's friends at the wake. Or maybe I did—it's hard to remember. The room was dark, loud, and I'd endured hours upon hours of conversation, small talk, memories, and condolences. Standing, sitting, breathing, nodding, and smiling, with his body in the corner of my eye. I hugged Gwen, I know. Shook hands with Oscar. But in my memory the other three seem far away, shadowed. Nothing more than the color of their hair.

It was the next day, after the funeral, that I truly saw them for the first time—the brunette in particular. She stood in front of the mausoleum after the service, black tights and black Chuck Taylors, a printed dress and a black cardigan. Her head was bent and her hair hung over her face, but I could tell by the shake of her shoulders that she was crying.

I'd been crying for days. I cried so hard after delivering the eulogy that I couldn't stand up to follow the casket down the aisle, and the church emptied out around me. I knew I was supposed to leave, that we had to follow the body, see it lowered into the ground, but I couldn't stop. My grandmother and mother slid into the pew on either side of me, wrapped their arms across my shoulders. I wailed and shuddered and gasped. I don't remember stopping, finally getting to my feet. But I must have, because there I stood, dry-eyed, outside the mausoleum in the bright white sun, watching the brunette cry. I felt sorry for her.

And I had another feeling. If someone had asked me to articulate it on the spot, I would have said I felt numb. Or maybe detached, like I was witnessing a stranger mourning another stranger's death. I didn't think anything of it at the time; it was only a moment. Now I think it was the first time I realized I didn't know Matt—at least not the way I thought I did. The brunette and I were both mourning, but I wasn't sure we were mourning the same person.

After the funeral we hosted a luncheon at a nearby banquet hall. There were dozens of circular tables and a buffet. My parents, my husband, and I had stayed at the cemetery longer than most of the other mourners, dropped flowers and fistfuls of dirt onto the coffin. By the time we got to the banquet hall, most of the tables were already full. A table in the middle had been left open for us. We filled our plates and sat down.

I expected us to be joined by family. Instead, seeing Matt's friends from New Brunswick standing awkwardly at the end of the buffet line, holding plates and scanning the room for open seats, Mom waved them over. The guy with curly black hair sat across from me.

"Matt was like a brother to me," he said, staring straight into my face.

I supposed it was intended to give my parents and me some comfort. I supposed it wasn't an uncommon thing to say at a funeral. Matt's friend Jasper, from Alabama, had said the same thing to my mother. The difference was that I believed him. He'd stood next to me at the coffin and hugged me while I cried. He'd been a part of Matt's life for half a dozen years. This guy had known Matt for, at best, only two years, and I'd only ever heard Matt talk about him once—after he was arrested for hitting a politician in the face with a pie.

I felt a burst of anger. *Oh yeah?* I wanted to say. *Well he* was *my brother, and he never mentioned you.*

"Thank you," my mother said.

"He was the only one who came to my trial, you know," the guy said, and then he launched into a discussion about his support of Palestine and some trip he took there. To dig ditches, I think. I wasn't really listening. I was looking around at the other tables, wishing any of those other people—those aunts, uncles, or cousins, those old friends or old colleagues, those people who didn't have pieces of my brother that I didn't have—had taken the empty chairs.

———

A few days after the funeral, I pulled up Matt's blog. His friends had been leaving posts nearly every day on the bright pink page with the message that blocked his entries. Long missives, snippets of memory, song lyrics, apologies, wishes for peace, condolences. Every one of them, explicitly or implicitly, expressed love. It made me feel marginally better to know that so many other people were heartbroken, confused, missing him.

There was a post from the curly-haired guy. He called Matt's funeral bullshit. He said Matt would have hated it. He invited everyone to a party in New Brunswick to mourn Matt the way he would have wanted.

The anger I'd felt at the luncheon reignited, exploded. I posted back that anyone who *really* knew my brother would know that he loved our mother and respected her faith, and would understand why a Catholic funeral was important to her. Anyone who *really* knew him would know that he would never have begrudged her that, much less called it bullshit behind her back.

The curly-haired guy removed the post and apologized. Sort of. He said he was sorry for his thoughtless remarks. He acknowledged that funerals were for the living, and that the service in Michigan had been meant to bring solace and closure to the family. Then he said everyone was free to remember Matt in his or her own way, and he asked that everyone reading be aware that the blog wasn't "a good forum for comments that might be offensive to members of Matt's family or others who knew him in different ways than we did." *We. Them. The Jersey kids.*

I hated the curly-haired guy for a couple of weeks. Because he was a jerk, I thought. Because he had the gall to think he mattered. But as more time passed, as posts continued to appear from names I didn't recognize, as I read about inside jokes, bars and bands I'd never heard of, I realized I hated him because he had something I didn't—the last two years of my brother's life. I hated the curly-haired guy because I was afraid he was right. Maybe it *was* all bullshit. Maybe I hadn't known my brother at all.

I had only gone to visit Matt in New Jersey once, for a weekend the summer before he died. He'd decided to stay and take classes instead of going back to Alabama, so Mom and I went to see him. He met us at the airport, and the three of us rode the train from Newark to New Brunswick.

During Matt's first two years of college, when he was in Newark, I'd constructed a mental picture of him there based on our conversations. His dorm room: cinder-block walls and bunk beds, posters and empty pop cans, the fire hydrant he and his roommate had stolen, the windows through which he could see New York City's skyline. His suitemates: a large, muscular Italian guy who played on the football team, and a pretty boy who was a dead ringer for Justin Timberlake. The campus: tall, modern buildings made of concrete, scattered amid shops and offices, the cohesion of the university a layer over the collective energy of the city.

But as the train sped away from Newark, as the clumps of buildings outside the windows gave way to clusters of houses, the houses to uninterrupted stretches of green, I realized I'd never imagined New Brunswick. He'd told me it was a more traditional campus, more isolated. I knew that he was living in an apartment by himself. But he hadn't told me anything else. Not who his friends were or where they hung out, what his neighborhood was like or how long it took him to walk to class. Then again, I hadn't asked.

The two and a half days Mom and I were there, the three of us toured the campuses: Livingston, Douglass, and Busch, each one sprawling up from the banks of the Raritan River. We hung out at Matt's apartment, a studio on the fourth floor of a timeworn building south of downtown. We went shopping at an antique store, took the train to Jersey City, and spent an afternoon with my father's brother and his wife. We ate dinner at Matt's favorite restaurant and had lunch with his girlfriend, Cecilia, a painfully shy girl with black hair and large, frightened eyes who broke up with him a few months later.

All the while I tried to marry my brother to his surroundings, to imagine him, without us, walking past the glaring aluminum sculpture in front of the Livingston Student Center, or over the covered bridge near Passion Puddle. I tried to picture him lying under a group of trees where students were stretched out with their books, at the Ethiopian restaurant or the burrito joint downtown. But I couldn't. It had been too long since I'd grounded him in concrete details, since we'd played out the dramas of our lives amid shared scenery.

The morning Mom and I left New Jersey, Matt met us at our hotel to say goodbye. He helped us put our bags into the trunk of the cab, gave us hugs, and stood at the top of the drive while the taxi pulled away. Mom and I turned and waved at him through the back window. He waved back—and then tore down the drive after the taxi, flailing his arms and jerking his legs, his mouth wide open. We couldn't hear him, but I knew he was making that sound he always made—a pulsing, falsetto sort of *AHHHH*. He chased us all the way down the drive and then cut across the grass to follow the taxi when it turned. I laughed so hard my eyes watered.

For several years after his death, I remembered that as the last time I'd seen him alive—running after our taxi, making me laugh until I cried, growing smaller in the window until I turned my head away.

Eventually it hit me that the real last time was about five months later, back in Alabama, at our parents' house for Christmas. For a week. But that was harder to remember, too quiet. He'd slept during the days, stayed up nights. He hadn't spent much time with us, hadn't wanted to watch movies or play cards. And I remember us laughing only once—when I opened his gift.

Over the summer, while Matt, Mom, and I were browsing in that antique store in downtown New Brunswick, I came across a cloth-bound, gold-lettered set of William Faulkner's Snopes trilogy. Matt had been a Faulkner fan ever since I'd introduced him to *As I Lay Dying* my sophomore year in college, so I made a big deal about the books, hoping that Mom would pick them up for Matt. She didn't get the hint. He did.

"I wanted Mom to get these for you!" I cried, wadding up the wrapping paper and tossing it at his head.

"Sorry to disappoint."

"No, these are great. Thank you. I'll send them to you when I'm done."

It was volume one I'd been reading, *The Hamlet*, when he died.

I tried hard after realizing my mistake to resurrect the actual last moment. What was he wearing, what was I wearing, what did he smell like, what did we say? There was a hazy memory of an early-morning hug before a long drive back to Chicago. Did it take place in the kitchen? The driveway? His bedroom? It was jumbled with every other post-Christmas departure of those last few years, when my brother, never one to get up early, would drag himself out of bed at 7:00 a.m. just to say goodbye.

This makes sense. The Matt who chased our taxi was the Matt I'd always known, the one who'd continually made me laugh so hard I went silent, gasped for air, clutched my sore stomach muscles, and fought to keep my bladder from exploding. The withdrawn, muted Matt at Christmas was the one I didn't understand.

Or did I?

In the first years after my brother's death, I equated that with-drawn, muted Matt with the Jersey kids. I was sure they had answers, secrets that would decode the various versions of my brother. I for-got that I'd witnessed Matt's quiet, shutdown episodes all our lives. I forgot how powerless I'd felt during those times, how there had been nothing I could do but wait for them to pass. Wait for the version of him I preferred: bright-eyed, big-hearted, full of life.

Because that's the reality of it. It wasn't that I didn't understand my brother's depressions. If anything, I understood them too well—enough to be afraid of them. To try and ignore them. To hope against hope that, each time they receded, enough of him would remain untouched to keep going.

I wonder if he felt the same way about me.

Over the years I have discovered that there were, in fact, secrets: parts of my brother's illness that I didn't understand, and truths that I wasn't able (or chose not) to see. Accepting that my brother shared different parts of himself with different people was one of the things that helped me through my grief. Trusting, finally, that I did know him was another. Coming to realize that there was enough room in his heart to love his family and his friends, and that his death didn't cancel out that love, was the last.

But first his suicide twisted his life into a question mark, tangling the desire to learn who he was with the desperation to understand why he died.

messages missed

After the funeral in Michigan and a memorial service in Alabama, my parents and I made the two-day drive from Tuscaloosa to New Brunswick to clean out Matt's apartment.

When Matt and I were growing up, every family vacation was a road trip. Four airline tickets would have been too expensive, especially since we went somewhere almost every year: Mackinac Island to eat fudge and ride bicycles on car-free streets; Denver to visit one of Mom's brothers and climb mountains; Washington, DC, and Pennsylvania to tour Civil War battlegrounds, monuments, and museums; western Michigan to spend a few days at the beach; Dallas to visit one of Dad's brothers and go to Six Flags.

Dad did most of the driving, though he and Mom switched off from time to time, and Matt and I shared the backseat. More often than not, my brother and I read books or played handheld video games, though sometimes we attempted Battleship or War. Dad put in tapes of Bill Cosby or Monty Python, and all of us laughed. Mom put in tapes of Phil Collins and Genesis, and Matt and I groaned. When we got older, radio time was chopped up into shifts—an hour a person, with some stretches of silence in between. That didn't last too long, though, just until Matt and I got Walkmans.

After we moved to Alabama, we drove back to Michigan for Christmas every other year. Twelve-hour trips that we did in a single day, the sky thickening gray with each northward mile, the snow evolving from twisting dust skittering across the pavement to

31

powder spreading on the windshield to mounds hugging the sides of the road. We always stopped at the same fast-food joints (a Wendy's in Franklin, Kentucky; a Taco Bell in Tipp City, Ohio) and saw the same exits for attractions (the Jack Daniel's distillery, the Corvette Museum) and towns with foreign names (Glasgow, Lebanon, Lima).

By then our trips had become quieter. Maybe we were lulled into boredom by the rhythm of the road, hypnotized by the wavelike rise and fall of power lines and the repeating landscape of trees, fields, and livestock. Or maybe it was just breathing room. The typical tension in most families with teenage children was a degree or two tighter in ours, given the difficulty of the move, and the onset of my depression and Matt's bipolar disorder. Still, even then the space that each of us occupied, the physical fact of our family, was a comfort. Four people moving through the world together, despite the fact that they were in their own seats, their own thoughts, their own skins. That silence felt elastic, capable of being broken at any time for any reason.

But on the drive from Alabama to Jersey to clean out Matt's apartment, a new silence replaced the old, hardened our separateness into something solid. It was the longest stretch of time my parents and I had spent alone since Matt's death, and as I stared out the window at the blur of Georgia and the Carolinas, the only voice I heard was a whisper in my head: *Think about anything but the empty seat beside you, the seat that was always his, the seat that will never be his again.* There was another whisper, too, quieter still, humming along with the rhythm of the wheels on the pavement: *gone gone gone gone.*

We stopped for the night in Virginia. Over plates of enchiladas at a Mexican restaurant near the hotel, we talked about how pretty the drive was, how nice the town was, how loud the music was. I smiled too hard and listed toward the middle of the booth, so my side wouldn't seem as empty.

━━━━━━━━

We arrived in New Brunswick midmorning the next day, checked into the hotel (the same one Mom and I had stayed at the summer before), and then headed over to Matt's apartment. There weren't any parking spots in front of his building, so we parked around the block and walked. It was unseasonably warm for May, the sun flaring off the chrome of the cars.

My uncle and aunt, the ones we'd gone to see in Jersey City when Mom and I had come to visit, were waiting for us at the front door. They'd volunteered to help since they lived nearby. Their proximity had been one of the reasons Mom and Dad had allowed Matt to go to school in New Jersey in the first place. He had struggled his junior year of high school, jumping from medication to medication in search of relief. A switch to lithium and a breakup with a girlfriend resulted in a suicide attempt by overdose the summer before his senior year. But a final medication change seemed to work, and his last year of high school passed more smoothly than any previous year had.

It helped that the Newark campus was only half a dozen miles from my aunt and uncle's house, so Matt had been close to them during his first two years. After the transfer to New Brunswick, he had been an hour's train ride away. Mom and Dad had worried about his moving, not knowing anyone and living alone. But he'd done well his first two years. He continued to see his doctor in New York and swore that everything was fine.

I made so many trips up and down the steep marble stairwell of Matt's building that day that it's hard to remember the initial climb. I imagine part of me was remembering the only other time I'd been there, the taxi-chasing-eye-watering-laughter. I imagine part of me was attuned to the possibility that the answers I craved, the something behind the nothing of the thank-you card he'd sent me just before he died, were contained within those walls. And I know that part of me, once I walked through his doorway, could not stop wondering where, exactly, he'd done it. That part was torn in two: half wanting, needing, to discover the spot; the other half wanting, needing, to run. To get as far away from that place as I possibly could.

We got straight to work. There wasn't enough room, or reason, to bring everything home, so we threw most of it away. Load by load we emptied the apartment, and load by load Matt's things disappeared from the curb. Mattress, blanket, and pillows. Chairs, bookshelves, and nightstand. I didn't think about what was happening, about how the space he'd occupied, the part of the world he'd carved out for himself, was being absorbed into other people's spaces. About how those pieces of him were being shifted into other contexts, wiped clean, and assigned new meanings. I didn't think about how a life could be reduced to boxes: a dozen cardboard, one burnished steel. I didn't think about anything. I trudged up the stairs, sweated. I plodded down the stairs, sweated. Up, down, up, down. I decided to take a break.

I grabbed a bottle of water and stood against the far wall, next to the windows. On one side of the room, my uncle sat at Matt's desk in front of the computer and burned copies of his files onto CDs. In the kitchen my aunt emptied out cupboards, her gauzy floor-length skirt tucked up between her legs. Normally her razor-sharp New York accent sliced through any nearby sounds. Normally her mouth was wide open, revealing two rows of perfectly straight white teeth and a laugh so deep and velvet that it almost eclipsed my uncle's subtle chuckle. But that day she was quiet. Everyone was quiet. Just like on the drive up, there was too much to say to know where to begin.

Next to me, Mom packed up the piles of Matt's books, folders, and papers. Since the mattress was already gone, there wasn't much else left in that corner of the room. Only the answering machine, still plugged in and sitting on the floor, a compact black box with a tiny red rectangle glowing on the front. Its unblinking eye was a reminder that my parents had listened to his messages two weeks earlier, when they'd come to claim the body. Mom had told me then that there'd been half a dozen messages from his friend Gwen, worried, wondering where he was. He was supposed to meet her at a party that day, the day he did it. It had been her birthday.

Outside the window, another family loaded up their child's belongings to return home for the summer, or to move on to one of those other places where students go after graduation. The block was full of them. I could hear the laughing and bickering, the complaints about the heat and the long drives ahead, slamming car doors and plans for dinner.

I put down my water, picked up a box of kitchen supplies—a few pots and pans poached from home, along with dollar-store plates and silverware—and headed down the stairs again. One of Matt's neighbors, a Hispanic woman, was in the foyer. I'd seen her and her daughters carrying Matt's TV and VCR from the curb back into the building, down the stairs into their garden-level apartment. I reached the box out to her, silently asking if she was interested in looking through it. She was. She took the box from my hands, set it on the floor, and unpacked it. She decided to take everything but Matt's toiletry bag. She handed the bag to me and reloaded the pots and pans. One of her daughters, a girl with a long black ponytail who looked to be about nine years old, came back up the stairs from their apartment and stood in front of me.

"Was your brother the boy in D2?" she asked.

"Yes," I said, looking over my shoulder at the row of mailboxes and door buzzers with the names underneath on sticky labels. There he was: D2, M. Schwartz.

"Oh, we were real sorry to hear about him," she said, and I believed her, even though she was smiling.

"Thanks," I said, and she nodded several times.

I turned around and worked my fingernail underneath the lower-left corner of his label, peeled it off the wall. I waited for something to happen—a wave of grief, a river of tears, a stab of pain. Nothing. I felt hollow.

━━━━━━━━

Back upstairs, I surveyed Matt's apartment. We were down to the essentials, the stuff that we would keep: clothes, records and CDs, the computer, the stereo.

The boxes of Matt's books and papers were still open and still against the wall. I stuck the label from his mailbox to the front of a black notebook, then pulled out and opened a lime-green folder—edges creased, corners curled. It was full of assignments from the creative writing class he'd been taking that semester, pockets torn from the strain of so many pages. Smooth, typewritten sheets and crinkled, scrawled-over notebook paper. I began to read, and it was there, in those pages, against that wall in that nearly empty apartment, that I caught my first real glimpse of the illness my brother had hidden so well. The drafts were choked with violence, detachment, and despair. Poetry and prose both surreal and sinister. All about violation, suffering, suicide.

Had his teacher read these? I pictured her keeping him after class, confronting him with her concerns. I pictured him laughing it off, chalking it up to an exercise in absurdism, an expression of the fractured postmodern self. I pictured her buying it, just like I would have, unable to reconcile the charismatic boy in front of her with the disturbing narratives. Of course he hadn't submitted them all, had he? Many of the drafts were unmarked. There was one piece that stood out from the others, the only one that didn't overtly touch on death or pain. Sanitized of red flags, public-friendly, it must have been something he shared.

It was called "The Life of Some Dude." Only two pages long, it was nothing but a sequence of answering-machine messages belonging to a character named Andrey Fetisov:

Message, 1, Tuesday, April 24, 4:28 p.m. . . .
Hi Andrey, this is Jan. Just wanted to see what you've been up to. We haven't spoken in a couple of weeks and I guess I miss you. Call me back when you can . . .
Beep!

Message, 2, Tuesday, April 24, 4:40 p.m. . . .
This message is for Mr. Fetisov. I'm calling with Comcast cab—
Beep!
Your message, has been, erased . . .

Message, 3, Tuesday, April 24, 5:01 p.m. . . .
Hey Andrey, this is Tom. Uhm . . . call me back? Uhhh . . . ok, bye . . .
Beep!
End, of messages.

Message, 1, Thursday, April 26, 10:17 a.m. . . .
Hello Mr. Fetisov, this is Lucy with Dr. Stern's office. I'm calling to remind you of your appointment tomorrow at 11:45. Try to arrive a few minutes early and don't forget to brush. Thank you . . .
Beep!

Message, 2, Thursday, April 26, 4:23 p.m.
. . . Click . . .
Beep!
End, of messages.

Message, 1, Friday, April 27, 3:54 p.m. . . .
Yoooo, Andrey . . . this is Tom. Uhm, somehow we missed it up until now, but Squash Bowels is playing tonight at Phantasy, . . . Cover is . . . six bucks . . . show starts at 10 . . . uhm . . . let's go . . . bye . . .
Beep!

Message, 2, Friday, April 27, 3:59 p.m. . . .
Hey . . . this is Tom again . . . uhm, show starts at 11, not ten . . . uhm . . . my bad . . . bye . . .
Beep!
End, of messages.

Message, 1, Sunday, April 29, 2:26 p.m. . . .
Hi Andrey, this is Jan again . . . still haven't heard back from you, so I wanted to see if I could catch you. Please give me a call back, the number's 334-555-3968. Thanks, bye . . .
Beep!

Message, 2, Sunday, April 29, 9:43 p.m. . . .
Shit, I think I left my wallet in your car Andrey, could you possibly give me a call and let me know when you get in? Thanks a bunch . . .
Beep!
End of messages.

Message, 1, Monday, April 30, 12:43 a.m. . . .
Andrey!!! Where are you man?? I need my wallet!! Get back to me!!!...
Beep!

Message, 2, Monday, April 30, 11:26 a.m. . . .
Hello Mr. Fetisov, this is Lucy at Dr. Stern's office. I'm calling about rescheduling the appointment you missed on Friday. You can contact us at 334-565-0892. Thanks . . .
Beep!

Message, 3, Monday, April 30, 11:34 p.m. . . .
Looo-ie!! Looo-ie!! Ah yoo commin' ta' da' pahty? Looo-ie!!!
Arrgh—
Beep!
End, of messages.

Message, 1, Monday, May 1, 5:20 p.m. . . .
Andrey this is Jan again. I know you're avoiding me, please just call me back, I want to talk to you . . . Please . . . thanks, bye . . .
Beep!

Message, 2, Monday, May 1, 5:20 p.m. . . .
Hey dude, it's me . . . uh . . . yeah, I don't know . . . call me back . . . bye . . .
Beep!
End, of messages.

Standing there in his apartment, in the shock of fresh grief, I didn't recognize "The Life of Some Dude" as an exercise in negative space, a narrative constructed solely by the reader through inference and interpretation. I didn't realize that it described exactly how I was feeling about my brother—as though everything I'd known about him was as clipped and small and insignificant as answering-machine messages. I didn't see that it was his story, a life constructed of missing parts. That the negative space, the mystery, the gap between what he shared and what he shielded, was part of who he was. Maybe part of why he died.

Years away from feeling whole enough to make connections, I didn't notice that the dates of Andrey's messages matched up with the dates of the last week of Matt's life. I didn't wonder whether Andrey was Matt, whether Andrey decided to die on April 30 after checking his messages, and if so, whose hand it was that pressed the button on the first day of May, whose ear heard those final two messages. A character with no name, no voice. A character whose questionable existence served no other purpose than to witness how quickly, how quietly, a soul escapes.

And I didn't think about those messages Matt missed, the ones on his machine from his friend, waiting for him at her birthday party—*Where are you, man?* I didn't imagine her voice shattering the silence of his apartment, temporarily filling the space around his soul-empty body. I didn't realize he'd chosen a time when he knew people would call, wonder—people who were far away, the party being in Newark. Somewhere to be and no one to find him. I didn't wonder whether he thought about how her worried voice would echo, whether he understood that we would be his witnesses, the invisible ears left to hear.

Years away from understanding the complexities of communication, I didn't realize that an understanding is a compromise. That messages encrypted or omitted are not the same thing as messages missed. That even when a message is clear, a recipient has to be willing, ready, to hear it.

Standing there in his apartment, I skimmed the poems and essays about death, destruction, and decay and stared at the gulf between the messages he spoke and sent me and the ones he left for me to find. I looked at "The Life of Some Dude" and saw a story about a guy who was avoiding a girl, who was trying to get over a breakup, who skipped dentist appointments and went to concerts with his friends. I looked at "The Life of Some Dude," and I saw nothing.

My mother was watching me.

"Did you see this?" I held up the folder. She nodded. I put the story back into the folder, put the folder back into the box.

The apartment was nearly empty. My father and uncle were dismantling the computer, my aunt was bundling electrical cords, and my mother was taping up the last of the boxes. Even though part of me hadn't wanted to look for the spot, I'd known from the start that I would. I'd been hoping for a minute alone to do so, a chance for private grief. But I was running out of time. So, as my family collected the last odds and ends, I began to search.

I thought about asking, but it seemed inappropriate. Morbid, maybe. Plus, I didn't know if my parents knew. I walked around the living room slowly, tried to be covert while my eyes scanned the ceiling—no hooks. I went into the bathroom, closed the door behind me, and tugged at the shower curtain rod—too loose. I circled through the kitchen, the dining room—no beams, no exposed pipes, nothing.

Then I saw them. Two large, bright nails, clearly brand new, shining silver with heads like dimes. Roofing nails, driven about an inch apart into the frame of the doorway between Matt's room and the kitchen. And I knew. I was sure that was where he had done it.

There it was, the wave. The soul-sucking spasm of grief I'd expected to feel down by his mailbox, that I felt every morning when I woke up remembering that he was dead. I wanted to collapse, to cry, to scream. I wanted to pull those nails out, hide them, bury them, burn them. They felt like a dirty secret I was ashamed to know.

The air in my lungs grew sharp, and my eyes darted around the room. Had anyone else seen these? Had anyone else seen me see them?

Nobody was looking at me.

I didn't say anything. I didn't want anyone to know what I had seen, even though in my heart I was sure they had seen it, too.

———

My parents found the note later that night, back at the hotel, while sorting through Matt's papers. It was written on the last two pages of his black Five Star Mead (the notebook I'd put his mailbox label on), buried behind outlines on the historical context of Marx, the guerrilla movement, and the Meiji Restoration. Behind a gender deconstruction of the movie *Fight Club*, drafts of short stories, and Milton Friedman's definition of economic freedom. Behind handouts, doodles, syllabi, and dozens of blank pages.

We'd flipped through some of the pages that afternoon but somehow hadn't noticed the end. It was 11:00 p.m. when my mother pounded on the door adjoining our rooms and cried out, "We found it. . . ."

I read it there, at the foot of my bed on the fourth floor of the New

Brunswick Hyatt. It began like a story, a detailed account of his trip back to school after Christmas. The difficulty of maneuvering luggage, disdain for his surplus of material possessions. The grinding pain in his knees caused by the stairs in his apartment building, and an anxiety so strong he struggled to fit the key into the lock.

And then it became the note—*hello and goodbye*. I read every word, and all but three slipped through the folds in my brain like a handful of water through the cracks in my fingers. I saw *sorry*, I saw *love*, I saw *sister*. Sister. Like he'd copied some template and forgotten to fill in the blanks. Like I hadn't even mattered enough to name.

I filed that memory of the note, those three words, away with the confusion and fear left by his creative writing drafts and the mystery of his blog (which I couldn't bring myself to read, even though it was accessible once we had his computer). Even when a message is clear, a recipient has to be ready to hear it.

I wouldn't read any of it again for over three years. Not until time, that true and beautiful cliché, had healed my heart enough for me to listen.

lydia

The morning after we found the note, my parents and I went to see Matt's therapist, Lydia. When we got to her office, she was waiting for us at the door—a tall, thin woman with cropped, stiffly sprayed hair the color of rust. Her face was lined and her eyes intensely blue. The first words out of her mouth were "I'm so sorry. I'm so, so sorry."

She opened the door and extended her arm, palm up, and we filed in one after the other. My parents sank into an overstuffed couch against the back wall, while I opted for an armchair. Both pieces of furniture were positioned to face an office chair that I suspected swiveled between its current position and the desk in the nook behind it. I could tell that the desk was strategically placed so that it wouldn't be obvious, just like I could tell that the office was decorated to create a sense of calm. There were plants in the corners, the floor was covered with patterned rugs, and the cinder-block walls were painted taupe and lined with large wooden bookcases. Shelves stuffed with books on psychology, literature, politics, history, religion. It looked more like a living room or study than an office, but I'd seen enough therapists not to be fooled.

Lydia took her position across from us in the rolling chair, crossed her legs, cocked her head, and fixed a thin-lipped look of concern to her face. Anxiety bloomed in my gut. It felt like an intervention, like one of the many family counseling sessions I'd sat through as a teenager. Only someone was missing, and really he was the only one who was supposed to be there. This place was part of his reality. He had stared into those eyes that were blue like flame, had looked at those walls, maybe flipped through those books. And he had said things.

Which was why we were there—to find out what he'd said. Find out the reason, even though we already knew there wasn't one. Not the kind of reason we wanted, anyway. We were looking for something that didn't exist, a replacement for the empty space he left behind, an answer that made sense. Something beyond *he was sick, he was sad.* We'd searched for it the day before in his shoes and shirts, records and books, canned goods and computer files. We had the note, but it wasn't enough. I didn't think anything would ever be enough.

My father cleared his throat. "We found a note," he said. "It looks as though it was written just after Christmas."

Lydia nodded. "Yes, Matt told me in January that he was having thoughts of suicide. He shared that piece of writing with me, and I asked him to sign a contract giving me two weeks' notice before attempting to take his life."

I felt my lip twitch into a sneer. I wanted to laugh. I wanted to ask her if her contract had ever worked, if her patients sent their notices by email or if they handed them in face-to-face, letters of resignation from life. Instead I said, "He should have gone to a hospital."

Her expression remained fixed. "I did speak with him about the possibility of hospitalization. He refused. He said he'd already been in a hospital and he would never, never go back."

"Yeah, well, he was in a locked-down juvenile psychiatric ward. I mean, there are lots of other kinds of hospitals. Hospitals with more freedom, with outdoor spaces. . . ."

"Yes, I discussed those possibilities with him as well. He refused." She turned to my parents. "I encouraged him to share his feelings with you after he showed me the letter, and he told me that he had."

I stared at my mother, eyebrows raised.

"Well, he didn't read us the letter or anything, but he said he'd been going through a rough time. That he'd really been struggling with the depression. But then he said that he was doing better, that he would be okay."

My head spun with adrenaline. "Why didn't you tell me what was going on?"

I was sure at that time, as I had been all of our lives, that I would have been able to help. That if given an opportunity I could have fixed anything. I still believed that my own struggle with depression qualified me not only to understand my brother but to save him. With the hubris of a firstborn, I assumed that my illness was his illness, as though he had inherited it from me like an old jacket or a too-small sweatshirt, and that if he had just listened to me I could have told him what to do.

"He told us he was okay," Mom said, looking beyond my head. "We didn't want you to worry."

Of course. I thought of all the times Mom had called me, urged me to contact Matt because he "wasn't doing well" or was "a little down." I always had, and every time he'd told me the same thing: he'd been depressed, but he was doing better. He'd told me he was okay. And I'd believed him.

I took a deep breath, hoping that some of my anger would escape on the stream of my exhale.

"I guess it probably wouldn't have made a difference," I said. "We couldn't have done anything short of flying up here and handcuffing ourselves to him."

"Even if you had handcuffed yourself to him," Lydia said, "even if you had forced him into a hospital, you couldn't have watched him all the time. Chances are, he would have attempted again. It's the nature of the illness.

"I believe his symptoms were present in his earliest memories," she continued. "He told me that when he was a little boy, the *Sesame Street* characters came alive on his curtains at night and threatened to kill his mother. He told me that a Shadow Man used to come into his bedroom."

"Nightmares," Mom said. "They were nightmares."

"I suspect they were hallucinations. It seems Matt has had a number of hallucinations over the years, particularly aural, most often having to do with music."

I wanted to be skeptical. My own years of psychotherapy had led me to scrutinize dealings with therapists for what I considered to be overzealous textbook application, the obsession with finding roots and definitions, categorizing symptoms and providing explanations.

I intensely disliked the notion of labels, particularly in a discipline so imprecise as the study of the human mind. Of course he heard music—he was a musician.

Yet something nagged. One of the pieces in the creative writing folder described these "hallucinations." It was a third-person account of a boy being tortured by a Muppet. The creature walked across the wall of the boy's bedroom, held up the disembodied head of his mother, and cut pieces off her face while the silhouette of a large man slipped past the door and into the room.

I remembered his cries, Mom taking down the curtains. I remembered being woken one night by a soft wail and opening the door to his bedroom, the light from the hall slanting in behind me across his covers. He'd whispered to me about the Shadow Man, his face red from tears, and I'd told him not to be afraid. I said there was nothing to be afraid of, that the Shadow Man was only dancing. And I began to dance, wagging my finger in the air like they did in the old Bugs Bunny cartoons that we watched every Saturday morning, my attempt at a Warner Brothers Charleston. I danced and laughed until he laughed with me, and then I told him to remember that when he got scared, the Shadow Man was only dancing.

Had I been wrong?

Lydia turned her bright blue gaze on me. "How are you handling all this?"

I crossed my arms over my chest, sank into my chair, and shook my head.

"Are you having any thoughts of suicide?"

An eruption of heat spread over my skin, as though I'd just been slapped. The residual adolescent anxiety I'd felt the moment we'd walked into her office, the indignation I'd felt at the absence of my name in the note the night before, and all the anger I'd been pushing down to protect my parents over the past two weeks finally boiled over. She was goading me, I knew it, and I didn't care. I wanted her to know I didn't care. I leaned forward, stared directly into her eyes, and said, "Every minute. Last night, when we found the note, I thought about what it would be like to jump off the balcony, to go and find him. . . ."

Smugness twitched the corners of my mouth into a smile. Then I turned my head, saw my father's horror-tightened face, the fear in my mother's eyes, and all my anger twisted into guilt. My mouth slackened and my stomach went cold. I looked at my parents, shook my head, and said, "But I would never. Never."

Though I wasn't sure if that was true. After all, I'd already tried it once. I'd tried it first.

homesick

It seems like the onset of depression should be gradual, a state a person sinks into, and I can see now that mine was. But it happened so slowly that I was scarcely aware of it. I thought—after the initial shock of realizing that my status as a "Yankee" in Alabama made me more of an outsider than a curiosity, after realizing that either my expectations or I would have to change in order to survive—that I was managing, coping, functioning at least. And then one bright, sunny morning in June 1995, a few weeks before my sixteenth birthday and nearly a year after our move, I woke to find myself fully submerged.

I was back in Michigan for a visit and staying with Leah, who had been my best friend since we were seven years old. It was the fourth time I'd been back since we'd moved, and each visit had been harder. Each time I'd returned I'd felt farther away, like there was more and more air between Leah and me, between myself and what I still didn't want to recognize as my past. The pot helped that. The day I arrived, we smoked up on a futon in Adam Reilly's basement. He was Leah's new boyfriend, a senior. I didn't even know him.

It was a weak high. The smoke tasted like pencil shavings, and the buzz only lasted a few hours. Afterward I felt even more alone. A stranger. A ghost.

The next day we passed a joint around a picnic table at Clements Circle Park, right in front of the public pool where Leah and I had spent summers turning brown on towels soaked through to the cement. I was sitting next to Nick Santos, and I couldn't believe it. I had pined for his caramel skin and long black curls during my freshman year. He'd never looked at me. Not once. And there he was right next to me, his fingers brushing up against mine, his spit at the damp end of the joint cool and wet between my lips.

This was the life I was supposed to have.

I could tell as soon as I opened my eyes the next morning that something was wrong. Consciousness trickled back to me but stopped short. I sat up, swung my legs over the edge of Leah's bed, and rubbed my eyes. Everything was out of focus, except it wasn't. Was it? Nothing looked right. The orange-and-brown shag carpet that my toes had known for nearly a decade, and the frameless mattress I'd slept on almost as many times as my own bed, seemed like props on a movie set. Nothing felt real. The walls, the dresser, the piles of clothes on the floor—it was as if the strangeness I'd felt in the presence of Leah's new friends had seeped into everything. Was I still high? We'd only smoked one joint at the park, and once again the high had been weak, lasting only a few hours.

The late-morning sun split the blinds and sliced across Leah's bed. She was already up—I could hear her and her sister, Denise, their voices mixed with the murmuring of the TV. Their mother had probably left for work hours earlier.

I stood, hoping the strange feeling was a fluke. That my brain was asleep, like a leg, and that if I just got to my feet, reality would return with the customary sharp pricks of "pins and needles."

Nothing happened.

I slapped myself across the face. In the half dozen or so times I'd gotten stoned, I'd learned that I was prone to panic attacks and paranoia. I found that a slap across the face made me feel sober for an instant, just long enough to remind me that I would be okay, that I wouldn't be (as I frequently feared) stuck, trapped, brain damaged, with a head full of cotton.

Nothing happened.

My heart started to beat faster. It had to be the pot—it had to be.

Was it some kind of mutant strain? Was it laced with something? I'd smoked strong pot once before, two joints' worth of a hydroponic dime bag that kept me high for twelve hours straight. But I'd never come down and gotten high again. Was that even possible?

Maybe I was being punished, I thought. God was punishing me. *I swear I'll never do it again, never, never, never,* I prayed. *Please just let this stop, just let me be okay.*

Nothing happened.

Leah and Denise are out there. Do they know I'm awake? What will I say to them? Should I pretend everything is okay? If it was something in the pot, Leah would feel it, too. She would feel it, and she would have said something to me already. God is punishing me. God is punishing me.

I have to pee.

Leah's bedroom was right across the hall from the bathroom. I knew if I made a run for it they wouldn't have time to say anything to me. I took a deep breath and told myself to act natural. I threw open the bedroom door and scurried into the bathroom with my head down. I closed the door behind me and saw my reflection in the mirror over the sink. I saw my reflection and realized I'd had this feeling before.

When I was nine years old. The mirror on the door of our old medicine cabinet was perpendicular to the mirror over the sink, and when I was nine I discovered that if I hopped up on the counter, brought my face within inches of the sink mirror, and then opened the medicine-cabinet door, a tunnel of Kelleys stared back at me, each one in her own mirror, the faces getting smaller and smaller until there was nothing but a black dot. And each was my real face— the reflection of a reflection, the way I looked to the world. Different from what I usually saw, it seemed lopsided, uneven. I stared at it until it was nothing, the way saying a word over and over and over again reduces it to a meaningless combination of sounds. I felt the endless space of infinity inside me, a stomach drop like the first hill of a roller coaster, that second where you begin to fall and it feels like nothing is there to stop you. I went numb all over, and it was hard to look away. When I finally did, I carried that feeling with me, moving into the hallway like a sleepwalker.

And I kept doing it, back then. Marveling at the strangeness of the feeling, trusting that it was safe to walk that edge, to stare into that void, because I learned that once someone spoke to me, once I heard the TV or the phone or the neighbor's lawn mower, I was instantly reconnected with the finite. Me again. Regular, one-face me. After a while, I didn't even need the mirror tunnel anymore. All I needed to conjure the blackest stretches of the universe's mystery was my reflection and some time.

As I stared at my face in Leah's bathroom mirror, I realized that now I didn't need either. I didn't have to conjure the space, because it was already there. Somehow infinity had found a way to creep in without my permission.

That afternoon I sat on the floor of my grandmother's kitchen with my back against the cabinets, twirling the telephone's spiral cord around my finger and leaking the first, nonillicit details to my mother.

"I don't know, my head feels weird. Kind of dizzy? Like"—*like being high*—"like I'm just sort of out of it."

"Well, do you have a fever? Or a runny nose? Are you sick to your stomach?"

"*No*, I just feel . . . weird."

She told me she was going to call a neighbor who was a registered nurse and then call me back. I knew it was no use. I was only biding time. I would have to tell her what I'd done eventually. But still, I hoped. Maybe it wasn't the pot. Maybe the neighbor would know something. *Please, God, I'll never do it again, I swear.*

Mom called back and said the neighbor thought maybe it was sinus blockage from the flight. She suggested I take some Sudafed and try to get some rest. I stayed at my grandmother's house that night, but I don't remember if I slept. I imagine that I didn't. I imagine that the same guilt that had plagued me all day continued through the night. I imagine that I prayed some more. And I know that in the morning, nothing happened.

My grandmother made me an appointment that day with her doctor, Dr. Mason. I figured he would run all kinds of tests, that my drug use would be so obvious that the word *marijuana* might well be spelled out in platelets under the microscope. So sometime before my appointment, when Grandma wasn't around, I pulled a Dixie cup off the holder on the kitchen wall, opened the fridge, and took out the pickle jar. I can no longer recall where I picked up the rumor that pickle juice can invalidate a drug test, but I was desperate enough to try anything. I told myself it couldn't be that bad—Leah did it all the time. Not because she had to, but because she liked the taste. At the movies she would order the twenty-five-cent giant pickle, the one that was twice the size of a bratwurst, and then with a grin she'd ask the kid behind the counter to fill up a small paper cup with the juice, causing me and anyone else we were with to grimace and shake our heads.

I unscrewed the top, and the smell of vinegar burned my nostrils. *Leah does it all the time.* I tipped the jar slowly, so none of the pickles would fall out, and filled the cup. I raised the cup to my lips, let the first trickle of juice touch my tongue, and gagged. I jerked the cup from my mouth and carried it over to the sink.

Leaning over the sink, I pinched my nose shut and sucked the sour juice down in one shuddering gulp. I crushed the cup in my fist and dropped it into the garbage can. My stomach gurgled. I hoped it was enough. It had to be enough. If I drank any more I would puke, and I figured that if it didn't go through my system, it wouldn't do anything.

When we got to Dr. Mason's office, my grandmother followed me into the exam room. Before I could tell her that she didn't need to be there, Dr. Mason was in the room, firing questions at me about my medical history and symptoms. At that moment my fear of getting busted for the pot was finally eclipsed by my fear that something was really, really wrong with me. And the possibility that I was stuck, trapped, a brain-damaged cottonhead whom no slap to the face or lawn mower could save, was too much. I had to tell him the truth.

But my pot-busting fear rallied. I simply could not narc on myself in front of my grandmother.

"Um, Grandma? Can you wait for me in the waiting room?"

I knew how weird it sounded; I was all but confessing by asking her to leave. But my grandmother walked out of the room without a question, without so much as raising an eyebrow. And as soon as she left, it escaped my mouth in a whisper:

"I smoked some pot."

"What was that?" Dr. Mason looked up from his clipboard.

"I said I, uh . . . I smoked some pot."

I don't remember the tone of his response or his exact words. All I remember is the momentary relief at having told someone who might actually be able to help me, mixed with shame. But I do remember the gist of what he said, that it was possible there had been something in the pot, PCP or another drug or some kind of chemical. He ran a urinalysis and came back with the results.

Negative. For everything. Even the pot. Dr. Mason assured me it wasn't because of the pickle juice. There was no choice then. I had to go home. And I had to tell my mother.

Another conversation on Grandma's kitchen floor, but this time there was no phone cord twisted around my finger. Instead my free hand covered my face, caught my tears, and funneled my words directly into the receiver so that my grandmother couldn't overhear them, even though I knew Mom would tell her everything as soon as I handed over the phone. There was less yelling than I'd anticipated (probably because I was already hysterical, and eight hundred miles away) but plenty of "disappointment." I was grounded, driven to the airport by my grandmother, and shipped back to Alabama on the first available flight.

While on the plane I hoped, halfheartedly, that my return would somehow fix everything. Surely my own house, my own bed, my own family, would dispel the strangeness.

But as soon as I got off the plane, as soon as I saw my mother's face, the feeling was still there. Coating everything. Inescapable.

———

When I woke up the next morning, still feeling cottonheaded, my mother took me to a drop-in clinic. We sat silently in the exam room, the minute hand crawling its way around the clock on the wall, the air heavy with anger, guilt, and fear, until the doctor breezed through the door. He called me Princess, smiled while he listened to my heartbeat and the air filling and leaving my lungs. He asked me what my favorite subject was in school and pressed his fingers gently into the hollow beneath my jaw. He poked a scope into my ear, up my nose, down my throat, and told me not to worry. He drew some blood.

Though it must have taken a day or two to be processed at the lab, my memory has condensed everything into a single visit. The doctor leaves the room with the vial and returns minutes later with the results: mononucleosis.

There was a moment of relief, infinity rendered finite by science—a virus, a reason concrete and conquerable—and the fear that I would be stuck, trapped, brain damaged, with a head full of cotton forever, dissipated. But then the doctor said, "There's something else." He turned to my mother. "I think your daughter may be suffering from depression."

Something happened.

Hunched at the edge of the exam table in the clinic, my mother speechless beside me, I felt infinity burst, flood into every corner of me and beyond, bleed out into the world, and swallow everything whole.

Q & A

There was nothing we could do about the mono, the doctor said. We'd just have to keep an eye on my spleen and let the virus run its course. For the depression he gave us the name of a psychiatrist, a prescription for Xanax, and only the vaguest idea of what his diagnosis actually meant.

The medical community likes to keep things biological, so if there had been a pamphlet to tuck the prescription into, I imagine it would have mentioned genetic predisposition and environmental exacerbation. There might have been an illustration of a neural transmitter receptor and little floating balls of serotonin, a list of symptoms, and an ad for Prozac on the back.

But there wasn't a pamphlet. No Wikipedia page or WebMD. Prozac had only been out for about five years, and I didn't know anyone who took it. I hadn't even read *The Bell Jar* yet.

Now I wonder why, facing something so unfamiliar, my parents didn't ask more questions. Or any questions, really. One explanation is that they trusted the doctor. Another is that they were stunned mute, that they'd discovered the once-solid world was made of glass and the slightest misstep, the smallest sound, would shatter it to bits.

Maybe they didn't want it to be true. Maybe they already knew unequivocally that it was and wanted it to be done, dealt with, as quickly as possible. Maybe they were afraid that *what* would lead to *why*, and *why* would lead to blame. Genetic, moral, spiritual, or emotional failures that were beyond their control or correction, and to list them, sort them, pile them, trace them, would amount to nothing more than torture. Maybe they knew it was pointless, that there were no easy answers. A smear of blood, in this case, would yield nothing.

Maybe they were grateful to have a culprit, even if it was one as shifting and shaky as depression. Maybe they made the mistake of assuming a diagnosis came with a cure.

If my parents had asked questions, or had taken it upon themselves to find some answers, the *DSM-IV* would have been the most likely source of information. The psychiatric industry's handbook for diagnosing mental illnesses at the time, the *DSM-IV* came out in January 1994, about a year and a half before my diagnosis. It says that the criteria for a major depressive episode, the main symptom of major depressive disorder, includes five or more of the following symptoms present during a two-week period:

1. depressed mood most of the day, nearly every day
2. markedly diminished interest or pleasure in all, or almost all, activities most of the day, nearly every day
3. significant weight loss when not dieting or weight gain, or decrease or increase in appetite nearly every day
4. insomnia or hypersomnia nearly every day
5. psychomotor agitation or retardation nearly every day
6. fatigue or loss of energy nearly every day
7. feelings of worthlessness or excessive or inappropriate guilt (which may be delusional) nearly every day
8. diminished ability to think or concentrate, or indecisiveness nearly every day
9. recurrent thoughts of death (not just fear of dying), recurrent suicidal ideation without a specific plan, or a suicide attempt or a specific plan for committing suicide

I go back to the exam room, in my memory, and try to picture myself the way the doctor would have seen me: a girl whose eyes were sunken, shadowed, and swollen from days of continuous crying. She cried while her blood was drawn, told him she was scared, tried to explain to him the loss of reality, the cottonhead. A girl with knobby knees jutting out of torn, baggy jeans, and stick-thin arms hanging from the frayed sleeves of a thrift-store T-shirt. Five feet, three inches, weighing ninety pounds.

I imagine the questions he asked and how I answered them: *How is your appetite?* Not good. Mom butts in to tell him that I complain of nausea, that I vomit often. *Are you sleeping?* I am sleeping. I sleep often, sleep long, sleep late. For the first time in my life, I drink sleep in deep draughts, write poems about the sanctuary beneath the covers. And yes, during the day I am tired. I think about sleeping, dreaming—the easiest, fullest form of escape. But I have mono, I'm a teenager—aren't I supposed to be sleepy, sensitive, moody? Aren't I physically and psychologically stretched to exhaustion by the work of growing? *Are you having a hard time concentrating?* I don't think so. Who can tell? School's out—what's there to concentrate on?

Do you feel sad? Angry? Do you want to hurt yourself? Do you think about dying? These questions would come later, when I finally met with the psychiatrist, Dr. Campbell, an owl-eyed Caribbean woman even smaller than I was. It was the earliest opening she had, and by then I'd been in a fog for nearly two weeks, the Xanax anchoring me to the couch, my eyelids too heavy to squeeze out any tears.

It's easy for me now, knowing how much worse it would get, to blame the diagnosis and the drugs for what would happen over the next few months, to forget what it was like then, in the beginning. The taut, steady pitch of panic screaming just beneath the layer of sedatives, the certainty that I would never feel anything but that fear and desperation. *Do you*—Yes. *Do you*—Yes. Yes, yes, yes.

A quick scratch of pen across her prescription pad, and I was introduced to Paxil, a selective seratonin reuptake inhibitor (SSRI), and Mellaril, an antipsychotic used in the treatment of schizophrenia and psychosis. She told me the former was in the Prozac family. She told me the latter would help me to "stay calm." What she didn't tell me—because she didn't know, because no one knew back then— was that there is a risk of worsening depression when someone starts SSRIs, especially for teenagers. The warning signs are agitation, aggression, anger, irritability, insomnia, and the emergence of suicidality (an increase and intensity of suicidal thoughts and inclinations).

Within the first few weeks of starting the medication, I stopped sleeping, even though I was tired all the time. I cried constantly, screamed at my parents and my brother. I slammed doors, broke things. When school started that August, walking up the stairs to my locker gave me heart palpitations. And thoughts of suicide—which had once been limited to *If I killed myself, they'd all be sorry*, a knee-jerk reaction to such traumatic occurrences as being dumped or fighting with a friend—became more about the fact that I couldn't stand the feeling of my own skin.

Though my symptoms sound a lot like today's warning labels, it's impossible to know for sure whether it was the meds that dragged me deeper or whether I'd have fallen anyway, was already falling too fast. Knowing that there was a possibility of worsening depression may have spared me the surety that my situation was hopeless, that I would decline steadily until I lost my mind completely, but it wouldn't have erased the past year, the tearing of my old life from my new. No label could have told me that the cotton-packed unreality was actually clarity, the first sharp understanding of everything I'd lost. Not just a place, not just people, but a life—the life I could have had, the person I could have been. No black-box warning could have explained how to let that life go without feeling like I'd lost everything.

Which begs the question: Is there anything that could have?

━━━━━━━━

I've spent the first half of my thirties learning that change is inevitable. It seems a little ridiculous to admit that. It seems like something that we, as human beings, should know by the time we have baseline cognition. I mean, I grew up in the Midwest, for crying out loud; the atmosphere itself—scalding heat, droughts, floods, tornados, blizzards, subzero deep freezes—screamed that nothing was permanent. But all I learned was that no *weather* was permanent. Despite all evidence in my life to the contrary—changes in my body, my friendships, my education, my home—I grew into adulthood thinking that eventually, if I just tap-danced fast enough, I could make the world stop spinning.

When I realized that I couldn't, this thing that I'd spent half my life calling depression, this scritchy rodent I thought would gnaw at my insides until the day I died, started to disappear.

I don't mean to make it sound easy. I am certainly not suggesting that I plopped down on a *zafu* and ten minutes later, voilà—sanity. It's a process that is still happening—probably one that always will be. What I mean to say is that losses, deaths, friends, hours of meditation, and tons of books on spirituality got me thinking maybe it was okay to ease my grip. Maybe it was okay to let the people I loved change, and the places, and maybe it was okay for me to change, too. Maybe I could try letting life move like a river and trust that the downs would come up again on their own.

And they did, I discovered—faster than they ever had—when I finally stopped grinding my teeth and trying to force them to.

The biggest breakthrough for me was when I realized that being happy wasn't the opposite of being depressed. I'd made myself just as crazy scrambling to hold on to my pleasant feelings as I had trying to push away my dark ones. Once I decided to stand still and feel what I was feeling, no matter what it was, life got a lot less scary.

So, back to the question at hand: What could have helped me to let go of my old life in Michigan without feeling like I'd lost everything? It's possible that a really, really amazing therapist might have been able to pound a little wisdom into my thick teenage skull. But I had an amazing therapist and I didn't want to listen to a damn word she said. The truth of the matter is that nothing could have helped me, because I *had* lost everything. I needed to be wounded. I needed to grieve.

But I didn't know how. That silent MYOB gene told me to hide the pain. So, like a cartoon character, I buzzed around, plugging emotional leaks as quickly as I could, until I was out of fingers and toes and the dam burst.

Which is what needed to happen. I had to fall apart so I could come back together. I've had to do it more than once. As far as I know, that's the only way I could get to be thirty-something and figure out that the literal and metaphorical seasons were going to cycle whether I wanted them to or not.

Before I understood that, I obsessed over the what-ifs. What if we had never moved? Would something else have triggered a depressive episode? Would I always feel this way? Was depression truly typed into my genetic code?

After my brother died, these questions ballooned into their own universe: a parallel universe made up of all the lives he might still be living, if only. If only we hadn't moved. If only he had stayed in Alabama for college. If only his girlfriend hadn't broken up with him. If only his therapist had contacted my parents.

There are an infinite number of these scenarios, one for every nanosecond that could have changed his life. The first few years after his death, this was the book I'd write in my head at night, when I couldn't sleep. At first there was always a fairy-tale ending: my brother on the right kind of meds, falling in love with a girl who loved him back, settling into a career that made him feel purposeful and positive, raising a couple of rambunctious, well-adjusted children. That fantasy stung, ached like a wound. But eventually other scenarios began popping into my head. Some of his friends in Michigan became heavy drug users after we left, and I saw him as an addict: overdosing, driving under the influence and hurting (or killing) someone, getting arrested, spending decades in jail. I saw him stuck in the same pattern he'd been fighting for the past six years, battling depressions so deep he'd spend the rest of his life bouncing in and out of hospitals. I saw my brother experiencing what he most feared: psychotic manias. I saw him disappearing for years at a time, requiring constant care when he returned, my parents fading to specters of their former selves.

I don't write these stories anymore. Not because I don't wonder about the lives that could have been, or because I think he made the right decision. I just got to the point where I realized that anything could have happened, but only one thing did. And it was terrible and sad and hard, but I needed to sit with it. To accept it. I needed to let it be what it was.

The same thing became true for my life. I'd spent years asking myself what if my parents or I had said no to the medications, had asked if there was another way? Then I realized it didn't matter, because we hadn't.

The pills had tick-tick-ticked against the plastic of their bottles. Our hearts had thunk-thunk-thunked against the bones of our chests. The days had one-two-three been checked off the calendar. And we'd held our breath, as if we'd known what was coming next.

charcoal

For a while when I was younger, before I was smart enough to realize that adults who say you can be anything you want to be when you grow up are just trying to build your self-esteem, I thought I would be an artist.

When Matt and I were children, our kitchen table was frequently covered with paper, crayons, pencils, and markers. We created alien landscapes and comic books, traced characters from our favorite cartoons. We both continued to gravitate toward art throughout adolescence, but during my freshman year in high school I started to take it more seriously. I took an art class where I learned about shading and depth, texture and space, and something inside me shifted. I began to see the world as angles and shadows waiting to be captured. I spent hours working in my sketchbook, discovering that I loved the way drawing made me feel. Peaceful, like the volume on the world was muted. Powerful, like I had complete control over something. And focused, like I had a purpose, a goal.

After we moved to Alabama, art became my refuge. When the voice in my head—the one that constantly reminded me how angry I was, hurt and alone, hopeless and empty, afraid—grew into a scream, I knew I could silence it in glistening ridges of tempera or acrylic, the swirl of color spiraling off the tip of a brush in water, the cool tack of clay.

My favorite medium was charcoal. I loved the hiss it made against the paper, how the grains released by the pressure of my hand tumbled down the page. They had to be handled delicately, the grains, blown away gently, because brushed with the back of a hand they streaked and smudged. Sure, the mistakes could be erased, but the space would never really be white again.

I loved charcoal's mutability, its possibility. One stick, if used properly, could yield every shade of gray and the deepest black imaginable. I pressed hard often, ground my pencils into the page, because I loved that black. It was pure, absolute. It was an echo of the darkness I felt growing inside me.

The only true self-portrait I ever created, the only one that wasn't asked of me but rose out of a nameless need, an urgency, was done with charcoal.

It was the start of my junior year—August 1995, less than two months after I visited Leah and was diagnosed with depression. When the memory begins, I am already drawing. Back hunched and head bent in front of the full-length mirror that hangs on the back of my bedroom door, staring up through my hair into the reflection of my eyes. I am cross-legged, and the sketchpad is balanced on the inside of my thigh. I push and pull the charcoal across the heavy paper, the scrape absorbed by the percussive stutter and sawing distortion of guitar coming from my stereo. It's a Nine Inch Nails song, "Dead Souls," and I have it on repeat.

I am lost in myself, the world dissolved, and nothing exists but these lines. My mind is clear, empty, but my hand knows exactly what it's doing, feels the shapes it leaves behind, has felt them since they existed—nose, cheeks, chin, lips—has waited sixteen years to press them into this page. I don't know why I am drawing, or what imprint I am hoping to leave behind. I have no conscious intention. Only the silent knowledge that it must be done.

Whether minutes or hours passed I don't remember, but I know there came a moment when the drive left me in a shudder and consciousness returned with a snap so hard it made me gasp. I looked down at the portrait. I'd drawn my shoulders upright, squared. My chin was lowered and my hair spilled forward, covering my temples and ears. The whites showed under the irises of my upward-glaring eyes, pupils filled in black, thick, flat. No shadows. No wrinkles. The white skin true space, untouched by charcoal or time. Eyes straight forward, forehead leading, as though I was about to charge into something, or someone, headfirst.

I couldn't believe I'd done it. Something about it felt special, shivered my core. Now, in my thirties, I know that I recognized in those lines the black infinity that had been scratching at the inside of my head for the last two months. It was the face that had been haunting me since I'd looked in Leah's mirror. What I didn't yet have words for, what I couldn't explain to my mother, my doctors, myself.

A few days later I showed it to the boy I was dating at the time, Christopher.

"Don't you think it looks *exactly* like me?" I prodded, eyes wide, head slightly nodding. I imagine I was holding my breath, and that an eternity passed during that second.

He shrugged. "It's pretty good."

Pretty good? He was crazy. It was a fucking masterpiece.

I didn't show it to anyone else after that. I knew they wouldn't understand.

———

Autumn in the South is more of a wishful thought than a season—summer's heat often ripples on into November. Yet as Halloween approached that year I defiantly donned long skirts, combat boots, and black sweaters. Dr. Campbell, suspicious of the heavy clothing given the mild weather, made me pull up my sleeves during our sessions to see if I was trying to hide cuts. I wasn't. I dyed my hair black, ringed my eyes with black eyeliner. I was trying to color myself in, or blot myself out. I was trying to make my outsides match my insides.

I'd been waiting almost four months for the pills that rattled in my bathroom drawer to fix the hole that had been leaking infinity, letting in darkness. But every morning when I looked in the mirror, I saw my portrait: my face a flat, hollowed-out mask, vacant and stark as a skull. All smudges and shadows. Nothing more than the idea of a person, sketched in ashes.

———

That afternoon in late October was like any other. Christopher had come home from school with me, and we were listening to music and drawing in my bedroom. My mother came to the door after a couple of hours and said it was time for Christopher to go home.

To a casual observer, it may have seemed that I attempted suicide minutes later because I disagreed. I started screaming, after all. Throwing whatever I could get my hands on, flinging an end table across the room, running into the bathroom and slamming the door behind me.

But it wasn't the argument. It was my reflection in the bathroom mirror.

The bathroom was dark when I entered, but there was enough gray light around the edges of the door for me to see the face. Pure white skin. Eyes black holes. Shoulders squared, chin down. Too much black to erase. I wasn't angry—I was broken. And I knew I would never be the same again.

Something happened in that moment. When I tried to explain it to doctors later, they called it "an out-of-body experience." I didn't argue, but it didn't sound quite right to me. It was more like I was stuffed into the back of my head, conscious but unable to control myself. When I try to remember it, I am there again, crushed small and stuck, voiceless, helpless.

I see the face in the mirror smile at me, hear the pill bottles roll and rattle as I open the drawer. I see a handful of orange pills that glow like sparks in the half dark, the only color in the room. I feel their weight on my tongue, feel them click against my teeth. Five thousand milligrams of Mellaril—nearly an entire bottle. I bend down and drink from the tap. One, two, three gulps of water, and all fifty pills are down.

I move as in a dream, slide from bedroom to hallway to living room to kitchen. My mother is there, her purse on the counter, her keys in her hand. Christopher stands beside her, shouldering his backpack. They stop talking and stare at me as I push past them and slide through the back door, the open garage, the driveway. The world begins to swim.

There was no flash of lightning, no hand of God, but somehow at that moment I got what I had been waiting for all those months. The

ocean of infinity drained away. Perhaps the overdose of antipsychot-
ics melting into my bloodstream helped my brain to locate my buried
sanity. Or maybe I felt it closing in. Over my shoulder. Death.

I am about to die.

Oh God.

The pavement met me halfway, grated my palms and knees. My
stomach clenched, and I stuck my tongue out as far as I could, felt the
spasm move up through my chest, my throat. A sucking retch, and a
mound of orange encased in a clear cocoon of mucus jiggled on the
white cement.

My mother was next to me, her voice as clear and loud as the one
in my head.

"What did you do?"

—————

There is emptiness here. A black bar like a prison-censored letter.
Maybe my memory is attempting to protect me. Maybe I tapped into
a fear so deep that I jarred myself out of the state of consciousness
where memories can be made. Maybe I wasn't thinking anymore,
only feeling. Feeling fear. Which would explain why I ran.

I was halfway down the street when the paramedics peeled me off
the pavement. I couldn't see their faces, I couldn't see anything but
blocks of color. One of them talked to me, though. He told me in a
calm, steady voice that everything was going to be okay. I might have
been crying. There was a cold spot in the crook of my arm, an IV. *I've
never had one of these before*, I thought, just before the rushing tide
of blackness pulled me under.

—————

The emergency room was white. I was in a bed against a wall, no
curtains, people everywhere. My mother stood next to me, alongside
a nurse who offered up my options: a clear plastic cup with an inch of
black sludge at the bottom and something that looked like a hot water
bottle with a coil of hose at one end. Activated charcoal or stomach
pumping, she explained.

"Yer lucky yer awake. Most folks don't git to choose. If I was you, I'd go with this one," she said, waggling the cup.

I brought it to my lips, and as soon as the grit scraped my teeth, I gagged. I told the nurse I couldn't take another sip. She shook the hose at me and poured some Sprite into the cup.

"Better drink it fast, or yer gonna get pumped," she said. So I did.

Then the nurse helped me from the bed to a wheelchair and pushed me into a small office. My mother was there, talking on the phone. She hung up and said, "That was Dr. Campbell. She says there's no room here. We're going to have to take you to a hospital in Birmingham."

What hospital? I wanted to ask. *Why do I have to go to another hospital?* But I was sleepy again, and the next thing I knew, the wheelchair was gliding across the parking lot. I tried to be upset, to protest, but my limbs were full of sand. I spent the first half of the hour-long drive asleep in the front seat. My body had never been so heavy. I was completely paralyzed.

Until the charcoal kicked in and I realized that the sand in my limbs had rushed to my stomach and was winding up my esophagus—fast. We pulled over at a Taco Bell. Black oozed between the fingers I'd clamped over my lips as I sprinted from the car to the bathroom, which was thankfully, miraculously, a single stall. I locked the door, dropped to my knees, and heaved over and over and over again, my muscles burning so hot I thought they couldn't possibly continue to contract, but they did and they did and they did and my vomit turned a watery gray and just when I dared to think it was almost over, that I couldn't possibly have any fluid left in my body, I started to feel it down below.

I pulled my pants down as fast as I could, spun around, and plopped down on the vomit-splashed seat. No time to put down toilet paper or a seat cover, no time to be disgusted by the wet slick on the back of my thighs. It was rushing out of me, exploding, splattering.

But not fast enough, apparently, because it started pushing up my throat again. The trash can was on the other side of the bathroom and the shit stream was continuous and I tried to cover my mouth again but it was no use—gray and black chunks sprayed out across the floor.

When it finally ended I stood, shaking and exhausted. I wiped off my legs as best as I could and stared at the charcoal vomit–covered floor, wondering if I should try to clean it up. But I couldn't. I had to clutch the wall just to make it to the door. The sand was gone, and so was everything else.

━━━━━━━

I woke up the next morning in the juvenile psychiatric ward of Birmingham's Baptist Montclair Hospital with no belt, no shoelaces, and fractured memories of my arrival. Another wheelchair, darkness. A nurse pulling my shirt up over my head, darkness. A young girl screaming in the hallway, darkness. Several staggering trips to the bathroom to empty out the last of the charcoal, darkness.

It wasn't until a nurse came and escorted me to breakfast (the waist of my jeans clutched in my fist to keep my pants from falling down) that I got a clear picture of my surroundings. The ward was a dim stretch of dead-end hallway behind locked doors. There were four bedrooms, each with two beds, a bathroom, and an unreachable rectangle of window covered by a gritty screen. The common room, or "activities" room, was at the end of the hall. It had a thin blue carpet, two large plastic tables (one rectangular, one round), a pleather sofa, a grainy television, and some bookcases choked with flattened board games. Its grated windows curtained the buildings of downtown Birmingham in a gray haze.

The activities room was where the nurse led me for breakfast. I sat down at the rectangular table across from the only other patient—Janey, a pudgy girl of thirteen with narrow eyes. She told me she'd been admitted in the middle of the night and was the one I'd heard screaming.

"They had to sedate me," she grinned over a plate of scrambled eggs. I didn't know what to say, so I nodded.

"Don't worry 'bout yer belt," she added. "You'll git it back soon as you see the doctor." She looked under the table. "Yer shoelaces, too."

I cleared my throat. "You've been here before?"

"Fuck yeah," she laughed, her eyes shrinking down to slits.

"Janey—language," the nurse warned from an observation cube at the front of the room.

"Sorry, ma'am," Janey said, before mumbling "fuckin' bitch" under her breath and rolling her eyes. "It ain't so bad. They make you do a bunch of stupid shit, and after a couple a days they send you home. Biggest problem is this fuckin' piss they call sweet tea. Gotta order ten extra goddamn sugars. You gonna drink yers?" she asked, eyeing my Styrofoam cup. I shook my head and pushed it across the table.

After breakfast I was taken to see the staff psychiatrist. I remember nothing about that meeting, except that when I got back to the ward my belt and shoelaces were returned to me in a plastic bag. I was apparently no longer a threat to myself.

And yet I was not free to leave. I had no power there whatsoever. And, for the first time in my life, I was completely alone.

———

By the end of the day, there were two more patients on the ward: Luke, a round-faced boy with freckles and an "anger problem," and Bobby, a tall, muscular boy with a drawl that sounded Texan and an addiction to hallucinogenic drugs. The next morning, Sarah arrived. With all four bedrooms occupied, she became my roommate.

Sarah was my age, quiet and thin, with long red hair that hung halfway down the back of her Pearl Jam T-shirt. Her wrists were covered with black rubber bracelets, and the ragged cuffs of her baggy jeans brushed the tops of her black Chuck Taylors. Though nervous, she seemed nice. We had the same taste in music. She told me how much she missed her grandmother, who'd recently died. She was the kind of person I could be friends with, I thought, until the lights went out our first night together and she started screaming about the devil—talking to her, stalking her, making his way across the wall. For the first time since the move, I found myself wanting to be with my family in Tuscaloosa. I resolved to do whatever it took to get there.

Which turned out to be three days of group therapy, role-playing, individual therapy, and occupational therapy. I got up each morning at seven o'clock, when the nurses turned the lights on, showered, dressed, and made my bed. I filled out workbooks and contracts, drew up "success" plans. I grew numb to Janey's constant defiance of authority and Luke's menacing stares. I laughed at Bobby's jokes and tuned out his rambling stories about acid trips. I kept a polite distance from Sarah and slept with a pillow wrapped around my head. I didn't have to be told the rules, they were obvious and simple: the more hoops I jumped through (even better if I could jump through them with a well-adjusted smile on my face), the faster I'd get released.

On the fourth day, I had a family counseling session. Off the ward, in a small room with dark blue walls, I sat at one end of the same kind of rectangular gray plastic table we had in the activities room, a shrink to my left, my parents to my right. Matt wasn't there. His best friend from Michigan, Sam, was visiting, so my parents had left him at home. He'd made me a card, though. My parents handed it to me. Plain white paper, a poem written in pencil:

To my poor sick sister,
that is very sad,
Yesterday you hurt yourself
very bad.
I love you lots and I
hate to see you mad,
Hopefully this card will
help a tad.
To cheer you up, I've
brought your favorite hat,
So you can look at it & say,
"I know someone named MATT"
So come back soon, Me &
Sam say "hi,"
If you want me to, I'll
pop him in the eye (cheap rhyme)
Matt
The man
with a plan,

peak of great-
ness, idol to mill-
ions, & of course . . .
Your brother that loves
You.

Kell, I love you, please don't do this to yourself anymore. I
know sometimes it seems like I hate you, but I never have, &
I never could, or will.
Matt (again)

I started to cry. I begged to come home. I swore that I had learned
my lesson. I wanted to live! I didn't belong there. The other kids were
crazy. *Really* crazy. I told them about Sarah's hallucinations, how I
lay in bed at night listening to her scream and cry, waiting for the
nurse to come in and give her another sleeping pill. I wasn't like that,
was I? I wasn't crazy, I had just made a mistake.

"Please," I said, "if you let me come home, I'll do anything." My
father's face was silent stone. My mother worked to look tough but
wavered.

"How do we know things will be different? How can we ever trust
you again?" she asked.

"You have to believe me. You just have to believe me."

This was the point of the family session, I thought. I had to be
forgiven in order to be released. Years later Mom told me that she and
Dad had wanted to bring me home after our session, but the doctors
had wanted me to stay another day. But back then, as a nurse led me
from the meeting back to the ward, all I knew was that I had failed.

telling stories

I grew up knowing the story of the fever, though it wasn't much of a story. Less the kind of thing we gathered around to hear about, more the kind of thing Mom mentioned offhandedly from time to time.

"Your brother got very sick when he was a baby," she would say. "His fever was so high I took him to the hospital. I was afraid he was going to die."

That was it. She never said what was wrong with him or how long he had to stay there, whether she brought me along, left me with Dad, or took me to a babysitter's house. For twenty years it was a three-sentence story: Matt was sick. He had a high fever. Mom was afraid he was going to die.

And then he did die, and she said, "I remember when your brother was a baby. He got very sick, got a fever so high I had to take him to the hospital. I thought he was going to die." She paused. "That's when it started, I think. He was never the same after that, I could see it in his eyes." She paused again. "And I didn't know what to do."

It was only a year or so after his death when she told me that. I was standing at my kitchen counter, the phone pressed to my ear, and in the silence I felt my heart beating slowly, steadily. I could imagine the fear and the helplessness that haunted her then, as a young mother, and now. Wanting nothing more than to save him, to protect him. Tallying her own catalog of failures, questions, and mistakes—just like I had been— all traced back to the moment she first felt as if she'd let him down.

I exhaled heavily through my nose and shook my head.

"No, no, I don't think that's how it works."

It's the chemicals in the brain, I told her. Little molecules floating around, crashing into each other, bonding, shattering. A sleeping dragon awakened by a hormone alarm clock. Not a fever.

"Not a fever."

Even as I said it, I wondered. Was it possible? Or was my mother so sure that fever was going to kill him, she never stopped believing it would?

━━━━━━━━━

I was released from the hospital a couple of days after the counseling session with my parents. Though it had felt like an eternity, I'd been on the ward for less than a week. After I returned home, my parents were strict, my interactions with classmates and teachers were awkward, and Christopher broke up with me. Minor changes in my medications (a cessation of Mellaril and an increase in Paxil) didn't seem to do much at first.

But then the next semester started and I made some new friends, caught up on all the schoolwork I'd missed, and joined the brand-new girls' soccer team. Little by little it became easier to breathe. By senior year I had a new boyfriend and I was set to graduate at the top of my class. I had been accepted into several colleges, had even won a few scholarships, and was dangerously close to being happy. Though I didn't quite feel the way I had before visiting Leah and being diagnosed with depression, the strangeness had subsided. The black hole still lingered, but the antidepressants had finally shrunk it down to a speck—a tiny drag that only seemed to affect my day-to-day life by threatening to reopen.

Matt was a freshman that year. Because the worst of my depression had been characterized by insomnia, screaming fits, and crying jags, my brother's moodiness, brooding, and tendency to lock himself in his room with the music turned up into the early-morning hours seemed like normal teenage stuff. Of course there was also the pot, but, again, in the grand scheme of juvenile delinquency, in a world where some of my friends did acid, mushrooms, coke, heroin, ecstasy, and anything else they could get their hands on, pot was not a big deal. I didn't know how often my brother got high, but I caught him one afternoon, alone, perched on the windowsill in his bedroom, exhaling a cloud through the screen. He begged me not to tell Mom and Dad. They'd already found his stash and forced him into an outpatient rehab program; he'd be in serious shit, he said—like, grounded-for-life shit—if they found out he was still smoking up. Wanting to be the cool older sister (and mildly enjoying the fact that I had something on him), I agreed to keep his secret. As a compromise, I made him promise never to do it in the house again.

One night near the end of spring—a couple of weeks before graduation, not long after I caught Matt getting stoned—a friend invited me over to her house to enjoy what was left of the mellow warmth before the inferno of a Southern summer descended upon us. We sat around outside with her sister and some other kids. A few people were drinking beer. I wasn't. It was dark, getting late, and I was supposed to be home by eleven. I said goodbye, got into my car, coasted down the driveway, and stopped at the road. Left and right, nothing but the dark. I started to make the turn, and headlights filled my window. In a panic I slammed on the brakes, the lights grew brighter—*don't they see me?*—and I spun in a shower of glass.

Somehow, then, I was standing in the middle of the street. The sky was as black as the steaming asphalt, and faces shifted between headlights and shadows. The crash had been so loud that my friend, as well as her parents and some of their neighbors, had heard and come down to the road to help. My friend's father gripped my shoulders and stared into my face.

"Are you okay?" he said, over and over again.

My hair, which had been tied back before the collision, hung over my shoulders and stuck in the pool of blood soaking my shirt collar. I pressed my hand to the side of my head, and when I brought it back down, my fingers were stained red. An ambulance came, and I lay flat on a gurney, strapped. Just before the doors closed, I heard my mother calling out. They wouldn't let her in.

I found out later that my friend had called my parents right after she'd called the paramedics. They followed the ambulance to the hospital, leaving my brother at home. After multiple X-rays and hours of waiting, it turned out I was only a little bruised and scratched—a miracle, considering I had been blindsided by a car going about sixty miles an hour. My parents were relieved, but they were starting to worry about my brother. They had been trying to call him all night to tell him that I was okay, and the line was busy. We got home around 3:00 a.m. and smelled it as soon as we walked in. We went straight back to Matt's room and opened the door. His stereo thumped, and he and two of his friends sat on the floor, enveloped by haze. The phone, in the corner, was off the hook. I raged at him in disbelief.

"What the fuck is wrong with you? I could have been dying. *I could be dead.*"

Here, in my memory, his face is hard and empty. The same face that will stare at me after his first suicide attempt two years later. Here, I think for years after he died, is the moment when I should have noticed that something was different. Wrong.

But I was young and I was me, self-centered to the core, and I was bruised and bloody and tired. So I told my parents how I'd caught him with a joint. I closed my bedroom door on the angry voices, got into a hot shower, and watched the dried blood run pink rivers down my legs.

Dad took him to rehab the next morning, and within twenty-four hours he was deemed suicidal and transferred to inpatient psychiatric care. Diagnosis: Bipolar I Disorder.

According to the *DSM-IV*, "Bipolar I Disorder is characterized by one or more Manic or Mixed Episodes, usually accompanied by Major Depressive Episodes." A Manic Episode includes three or more of the following symptoms:

1. inflated self-esteem or grandiosity
2. decreased need for sleep (e.g., feels rested after only three hours of sleep)
3. more talkative than usual or pressure to keep talking
4. flight of ideas or subjective experience that thoughts are racing

5. distractibility (i.e., attention too easily drawn to unimportant or irrelevant external stimuli)
6. increase in goal-directed activity (either socially, at work or school, or sexually) or psychomotor agitation
7. excessive involvement in pleasurable activities that have a high potential for painful consequences (e.g., engaging in unrestrained buying sprees, sexual indiscretions, or foolish business investments)

A Mixed Episode is defined as a period of time in which the criteria for a Manic Episode and a Major Depressive Episode overlap. As a result "the individual experiences rapidly alternating moods (sadness, irritability, euphoria) . . . agitation, insomnia, appetite dysregulation, psychotic features, and suicidal thinking."

The *DSM-IV* doesn't specifically mention the heightened likelihood of suicide during a Mixed Episode. But Kay Redfield Jamison, a professor of psychiatry who has bipolar disorder, does. In her book on suicide, *Night Falls Fast*, Jamison says that Mixed Episodes often bridge the transition from a Major Depressive Episode into Mania or "normal" functioning. This "resurgence of will and vitality," she writes, "makes possible the acting out of previously frozen suicidal thoughts and desires." Jamison also says that bipolar illness is generally more severe than depression alone, and while "one person in five with major depression will attempt suicide . . . nearly one-half of those with bipolar disorder will try to kill themselves at least once."

I knew none of this before Matt's death. Hindsight is proverbially twenty-twenty, so I see it now—the days he went without sleeping, the days he could barely drag himself out of bed. His constant need to wrestle, with anyone, often to the point of serious injury. The guilt complex that, he said, was bigger than his own comprehension.

But he and I never talked about his diagnosis. I didn't think we had to. As far as I knew, bipolar was the current trendy mental illness, the new depression, and by the time he was diagnosed I'd already blazed that trail: two years of therapy, psychiatry, meds, and a hospitalization. He was copying me, like he had our whole lives. When I'd started wearing flannel shirts, he'd started wearing flannel shirts. When I'd started listening to Pearl Jam, he'd started listening to Pearl Jam. When I'd bought Chuck Taylors, he'd bought Chuck Taylors. He was obviously jealous of all the attention that I'd gotten after my diagnosis. It was his turn to be crazy.

As far as I knew, *bipolar* was just his new word for my old problem—fucked up. But I was okay, so he would be okay, too. No need to talk about it. End of story.

———

Unlike me, my father didn't have to reach into hindsight to find his realization of Matt's illness. On the night of my accident, he felt the force of the change as it unfolded, as strong and sudden and spinning as the crash.

"I will never forget," he told me, "walking into that room at three in the morning and seeing him lying in bed. His friends were sitting on the floor, and I kicked them out. But your brother was so high, he couldn't move. And that's when I started to think something was really, really wrong."

But retrospection led him back further. The first stirrings of Matt's problems were months before the crash, when Mom found his pot stash hidden in a shoebox and my parents enrolled him in the outpatient drug rehab program. He met with a psychologist there, who then referred him to a psychiatrist. The first diagnosis was depression. He was given Prozac, which he covertly dropped into the toilet every morning, until a visiting uncle alerted my parents to the clump of half-disintegrated pills clinging to the bottom of the bowl in the guest bathroom.

I remembered none of this.

"So, did the diagnosis of depression worry you at the time?" I asked.

"I think . . . I just didn't want to believe that it was an illness," Dad said. "I thought he was going through a tough time, still adjusting to the move, trying to find his place. I was sure he would get through it. I wanted to believe he wouldn't have to walk that path."

The day after the crash was a Sunday, my father remembered. He had to go back to the scene of my accident in the morning to meet the tow truck driver and follow the crumpled shell of my car to the junkyard, where they paid him fifty dollars for it. He spent the rest of the day trading phone calls with Matt's psychologist, psychiatrist, and an inpatient drug rehab center in Birmingham. He dropped Matt off at the rehab center the next morning, where my brother was promptly transferred to inpatient psychiatric care and diagnosed with bipolar disorder.

Remembering my own reaction to Matt's diagnosis, I asked, "Were you surprised—or, I mean, did you believe them?"

"Yes and no. I was . . . skeptical. The depression I saw, he was so withdrawn. But mania? I mean, his doctors were asking us what his mania was like, and I kept telling them I didn't see it. I challenged the diagnosis a few times, when Matt wasn't around. But all the doctors he saw agreed. Of course, when I think about it now, I remember all those nights he didn't sleep. He'd stay up all night, working on his music. He'd get so excited about something that he'd drag you in from another room to listen to it."

I thought about the fever, his therapist Lydia's suggestion of hallucinations.

"Did you ever think, when Matt was little, that there was something wrong with him, something different?"

My father paused.

"He was so internalized. Quiet. But I always interpreted that as steadiness. Like he was dealing with things silently, but dealing with them. He was such a feeling kid, nurturing, empathetic. I always thought it was his character. I never suspected anything more."

Because Matt had been checked in with suicidal ideation, and because he was starting several new psychiatric medications, he spent nearly a week in the hospital after his diagnosis. He came home on a cocktail of meds, which expanded and evolved over the next two years: SSRIs, mood stabilizers, antiseizure medications. No matter what anyone did—my parents, his psychiatrist, his therapist—he couldn't seem to stabilize.

In the meantime, I had enrolled at the University of Alabama. During the two years that Matt struggled to find his balance, I made the dean's list and moved into an apartment near campus. I met and fell in love with my future husband, Ryan, a smart, athletic finance major who also happened to be from Michigan. I made friends, played club sports, went to parties and concerts, worked at a deli and a dry cleaner.

In July 1999, almost four years after my attempt, I was starting to taper off the Paxil, was set to finish my bachelor's degree in literature a year early and graduate with honors, and Ryan and I had decided to move in together.

In July 1999, two years after his diagnosis, my brother ingested a potentially lethal dose of lithium.

He'd been in the hospital for a weekend before the attempt, in order to transition from his cocktail onto lithium. He hated being on so many different drugs, especially when it seemed like none of them were working, and since a breakup with a girlfriend (a quiet, petite pixie who'd cheated on him and left him) had plunged him into a deep depression, it seemed like a good time for a change. According to my parents, Matt liked the idea of stopping the cocktail but didn't want to go to the hospital again. Unfortunately, there was no choice. The cessation of the cocktail would likely cause withdrawal, plus the lithium levels in his blood needed to be closely monitored, as lithium can quickly change from therapeutic to toxic. Matt relented but asked that he not be subjected to the strict regimen and regulations he'd experienced the first time he'd been hospitalized—likely the same the barrage of therapy and activities I'd endured. His doctors agreed, and he was allowed to leave the hospital twice: once to go see a movie, and once to go out to dinner with our parents. Mom and Dad brought him home believing that the transition had been successful. Less than a week later, he swallowed all of his pills.

He'd inherited my old bedroom by then. The move made sense— my room was bigger and had a private bathroom. I never asked him about his attempt, because I assumed I'd already experienced it. In the movie in my mind, he kept his pills in the same drawer where I kept mine. He swallowed them in front of the mirror, as I did. It wasn't until years after his death, not until I started writing about it, that I learned the details from my parents.

It was the middle of the night. He dialed his ex-girlfriend's number after he took the pills—not to be saved, just to say goodbye. To make her feel sorry.

The girl panicked and handed the phone off to her father, who then ordered my brother to turn the phone over to my parents. For some reason, Matt complied: he padded slowly down the dark hallway, opened their bedroom door, and handed my mother the phone. He saved his life that night by calling that girl. An important lesson for the future. A mistake he would not repeat.

His ex-girlfriend's father told Mom what had happened, and Mom hung up the phone. She dragged Matt into the bathroom, bent him over the sink.

"Throw up," she said. "Throw up now."

He did. Dad called the psychiatrist, who told them to forgo 911 and take my brother to the emergency room themselves, as it would be faster. They left immediately, with a bucket in the car, urging Matt to continue vomiting on the way.

This was the point where my parents' stories diverged.

According to Mom, the ER staff gave Matt the same choice they gave me: charcoal or stomach pumping. He chose charcoal, though she doesn't remember him throwing up.

According to Dad, they pumped his stomach. He says my brother was scared and he was standing next to Matt, holding his hand. A nurse came and told Dad he needed to sign some papers, and when Dad tried to go, Matt begged him to stay.

"Please," he said, "please don't leave me."

But the nurse said Dad had to, and when he came back, the tube had already been threaded into my brother's nose.

When I told Mom that Dad's version was different, I could practically hear her shrug over the phone.

"He has a good memory," she said. "Listen to him."

When I told Dad that Mom's version was different, that she remembered Matt's having been offered, and having made, the same choice I had, he paused.

"Well, it isn't always easy to separate your stories."

My parents agreed on the rest. Matt's blood was monitored all night, checked every fifteen minutes to see what kind of damage was being done to his kidneys. Mom and Dad watched the concentration of lithium in his system rise, having been told by doctors that if it reached a certain level they wouldn't be able to save him. Matt's eyes were dull, vacant. He was empty.

But by morning the lithium levels had fallen and he was released. My parents drove him to Birmingham and checked him back into the psychiatric ward.

███████

Toward the end of Matt's weeklong stay, my parents and I drove to the hospital in Birmingham to participate in the requisite session of family therapy. Before leaving the house, I went into the guest room (where all the old bedroom furniture, clothes, and random junk that wouldn't fit into my apartment had ended up) and rummaged through my desk drawers until I found what I was looking for—Matt's card. The one he'd made me when I was hospitalized. I went into the office, grabbed a yellow legal pad, tore a strip off the top sheet, and wrote:

> Matt,
> I hope you can remember this, and believe that I do know how you feel. And now I know how you felt. I just hope that something will awaken you to how good your life really is, and how many people care about you.

I didn't sign it.

I stuffed the slip of paper into the card, stormed into the garage, and slid into the backseat behind my parents. We rolled down the driveway, out of the subdivision, and onto the interstate. I set my jaw and fumed. Didn't he remember what my suicide attempt had done to our family? How could he have done this to our parents again? Had he learned nothing? Outside the window streamed a steady blur of kudzu-covered trees, the numbers on the exit signs climbed higher, and a Taco Bell slipped by. A seed of guilt pricked my stomach. Yes, he had learned. He had learned to take a bottle of pills when life got hard, and I was the one who'd taught him.

We pulled off the interstate and into the parking deck. He wasn't in the same hospital I had been in, but it didn't matter. The hospital, the psych ward, it was the same white dungeon—the hum of the lights, the squeak of nurses' shoes, and the blank stare of drugged teenagers. A young African American boy, twelve or thirteen years old, caught my gaze and started mumbling. The guilt and anger from the car ride vanished, and panic shot up from my stomach. I was sixteen again.

Memory engulfed reality, Then weaved with Now, and the room for Matt's family therapy was exactly the same as the room for mine: dark blue, with fluorescent lighting, a rectangular table, a doctor to my left, and my parents to my right. I wanted to beg and cry all over again. *Please I'll do whatever it takes just get me out of here just let me . . .*

The past receded like a tide. It was not my turn to confess, not my turn to ask for forgiveness. The faces were pointed at the other end of the table, at Matt, slumped down in his chair with his arms across his chest. Returned to the present, memory nothing more than a faint line in the sand, I felt the prick of the guilt seed return and bring with it the heat of anger. I hated myself for what I had done, and I hated him for doing it again.

With a flick of my wrist, I sent the card sliding across the table in his direction. I told him I was disappointed in him for doing this, knowing what it had done to all of us before. I told him to remember, to take his own advice. I waited to see a look of understanding, remorse. I waited to hear it all again, to see my sixteen-year-old self through my twenty-year-old eyes. I waited.

But he didn't cry. He wasn't sorry. Arms across his chest, eyes like wet steel. His face hard, removed, distant. No response. Only crossed arms. Only steel eyes. Only silence.

———

The stories we told about Matt said more about us than they did about him. Mom wanted the cause of his illness to be pinpoint-able, concrete, and beyond her control. Dad didn't want him to be ill at all. They told these stories out of love. Out of fear. Out of a need to keep him safe.

It was for the same reasons that I imagined Matt's first attempt as an echo of my own, that I couldn't acknowledge his stony face and silence in the hospital afterward. "It isn't always easy to separate your stories," my father said. I know what he meant. Details get tangled, erased, and rewritten over time. When the mind holds memories of two similar situations, there's bound to be some overlap. But for me it was literal. Our stories were twin strands, a double helix I had to weave together. Because we had to be the same. I was okay and he needed to be okay. He would be okay.

End. Of. Story.

three years

need

We spent the entire month of May 2004 dealing with the business of my brother's death. There was the body to retrieve; the casket, headstone, and plot to purchase; the wake, the funeral, the luncheon. There were homes to return to—I to Chicago, my parents to Alabama—and the second round to gear up for. There was my trip from Chicago to Tuscaloosa and the photo collage to construct for the memorial service at my parents' church. There were a couple hundred hugs and hands to shake. There was the drive from Alabama to Jersey to clean out Matt's apartment and pick up his diploma. There was the loading of boxes and another memorial, in a classroom at Rutgers. There was the drive back and the final flight home.

And then there was June.

My parents went back to work, Ryan went back to work, and so I got up early one morning, made a sandwich, put it and a book in my purse, and walked to the train. Just like I'd done every weekday morning before Matt died.

As I rode the Brown Line south toward downtown, toward the library where I'd started working as an archiving assistant after I finished grad school, I watched the familiar progression of trees growing smaller and buildings taller. *Today is a day,* I told myself, *just like any other day. This is life going on. This is what you need. The routine to return to while you pick up the pieces.*

I got off the train at the usual stop, walked the usual sidewalk among the usual strangers. I cut the usual circle to the back of the library, swiped my ID at the door, and punched the button for the elevator.

I wonder now what would have happened if I'd made it into the elevator alone. Maybe if I'd traveled up to the second floor, wound my way to my desk, and sat down at my computer without seeing anyone, I could have slid into that old routine. Maybe I could have convinced myself that I alone contained the change. I wanted desperately for the difference to remain within my skin.

But as I stood waiting for the elevator, I heard the door open behind me. I turned around and saw a coworker, a friend. And there it was on her face, the change I'd been hoping to hold in spilled over and spread. Fear, pity, concern—whatever it was in her eyes, it was different. And I would see it all day, every day, if I stayed.

I burst into tears. She dropped her bag and put her arms around me. I went home.

My boss called me later and said I could take more time, I could take as much time as I needed. I didn't know how to explain to her that the forward progress of time would not fix this. I didn't know how to tell her there was no room for After among the relics of Before. So I said thanks, and then I quit.

June turned into July, shock lingered, and survival boiled down to social-studies basics: water, air, food, sleep, clothing, shelter, and sex.

Water wasn't a problem, of course. Neither was air, technically, though my lungs, whenever I thought about my brother's lungs, stopped short of filling. A thin stream of oxygen squeezed through a closing throat.

I had the opposite problem with food. I craved salty, sweet, and greasy, cooked thick stews and creamy pastas, ordered deep-dish pizzas and Thai curries. I had triple helpings and then moved on to nearly burnt bags of microwave popcorn and sleeves of store-bought cookies dipped in peanut butter. Unlike my parents, who had given up eating altogether and were melting down to bones, I gained five pounds. Ten. Fifteen.

For sleep I had a steady supply of pills (courtesy of my psychiatrist) that consistently closed my eyelids for nine hours a night. Clothing and shelter depended on money, which we had enough of thanks to Ryan's job. Sex happened, though I'm not sure when I started to think about it again, how much time lapsed between thought and execution, and what, if anything, it meant to either of us.

Matt's death had drawn a curtain between my husband and me, between me and the rest of the world. Though Ryan tried (the question of my need constantly on his lips: *What can I do for you? How can I help?*), there wasn't much he could do, or much I believed he could do. He walked the dog and cleaned the bathroom. He handed me the remote control. He let me push him away.

July turned into August, shock faded, and survival became a matter of managing emotions. Rejoining the world. Discovering the clearest, easiest, path through (or around) grief.

I started seeing a therapist who specialized in suicide loss. I got a job teaching composition at a local community college and signed up for photography classes. I dropped acquaintances and avoided old friends. *This*, I told myself, *this is what you need. A different routine for a different life. One populated by people who didn't know the other you, who don't need to know about him.*

I fantasized about hopping on a plane to New Orleans, Miami, Paris, Alaska. Disappearing into a crowd, changing my name, and living the rest of my life without a single person knowing what I'd lost. Knowledge was the problem; the concern and helplessness I'd seen in the eyes of my coworker and my husband, the anxiety tightening my parents' voices during our telephone conversations.

They called me every day. We stretched small talk into hours—the lives of other family members, current events, sports, movies, and TV shows. We knowingly recycled news and anecdotes, pretended we were hearing the repeated information for the first time. We lapsed into awkward silences yet couldn't bring ourselves to hang up.

I told my therapist they were driving me crazy. He said I should tell them I needed a little space. I did, but the first day the phone didn't ring, I found myself calling them. They didn't say anything about it. The real reason for our conversations, though unspoken, was understood: we each needed to know that the other was still alive.

They spoke of Matt every now and then. Accidentally, it seemed— the usually innocuous flow of our conversation suddenly twisting, breaking into a torrent of grief and memory that spun and slammed me, left me weak and exhausted. I hated to talk about him. Saying or hearing his name, seeing his picture or his possessions, created a vacuum in my chest, a black hole that pulled at my guts and bones until I felt the force of it would literally tear me apart. So because I couldn't run off to New Orleans, Miami, Paris, or Alaska, because I knew even as I fantasized that leaving wouldn't fix it either, because I didn't really want to leave, to lose even more of the people I loved, I decided silence was what I needed—the complete and total absence of sound, at least where my brother was concerned. If I were inside the vacuum, then the vacuum would no longer be inside me.

But that was ridiculous. I couldn't pretend he'd never existed, and that the end of his existence wasn't impeding the continuation of mine. I needed to talk about him, to try to understand why he'd done what he'd done. I told myself I couldn't do that with my parents, because, while we shared Matt's death, we hadn't lost the same person. They'd lost a son. I was the only one who'd lost a brother—the only other person on the planet made from the same two people as I was, from the same past. What I needed was another twenty-five-year-old-girl who'd lost her only sibling. A girl who'd fought her own battle with mental illness throughout her teens. Who'd attempted suicide. Who, a few months after her brother's death, had stopped cold on the second page of the first chapter of Kay Redfield Jamison's *Night Falls Fast*, when she'd read the line "humans learn, to considerable extent, through imitation. Suicide, dangerously, has a contagious aspect."

That September I joined a ten-week suicide-survivor support group, to find myself in someone else.

The support group met in a crumbling brick building west of the Loop. On the night of our first meeting, a security guard directed me to the second floor, through a maze of hallways and offices, to a beige conference room furnished with folding chairs and a card table piled with cookies.

There were a dozen of us, plus the facilitators (a counselor and two women who'd lost loved ones to suicide many years ago). One by one, people introduced themselves and their losses—deaths by hanging, guns, pills. There were middle-aged parents who'd lost teenage and adult children, a fortysomething-year-old man who'd lost one of his several brothers, a thirty-something-year-old woman who'd lost her older sister, a girl my age who'd lost her father, and another girl my age who'd lost her younger brother. She was it, I thought to myself during her introduction, the double I'd sought. But the more she talked, the more I realized our stories were different. She had another sibling, a sister. Her brother had been an addict. And she said nothing to indicate that she'd had any troubles of her own, no suggestion that she'd done anything to damage him.

It was a sinking feeling, at first, but then I decided that maybe I didn't need someone just like me. Maybe all I needed was other survivors. Strangers. Easier to talk to than my husband or my parents, because our losses didn't overlap. Their dead (and mine) were once removed, buffered, shaped by their stories and theirs alone.

The lines from *Night Falls Fast* still echoed in my mind then, a reverberation under my consciousness like a struck tuning fork. I was sure that my attempted suicide had led to Matt's death, and that the people who'd known us, really known us (my parents, my husband, my closest friends), agreed. Over the next few weeks, I told the support group how I missed Matt. I told them I was angry. I cried. I told them what he'd been like: ridiculously, enviably intelligent; sensitive and empathetic; talented and creative. I told them how many people loved him, how many lives he'd touched. But I didn't tell them about myself, my depression, that my guilt extended beyond losing touch with my brother and failing to see the signs of his descent.

I didn't want them to know it was my fault. I needed to convince them that my brother had loved me, that we'd loved each other. Because if they believed it, then it would be true. And if it was true, maybe I could be forgiven.

The last five weeks of our support-group meetings, we took turns bringing in pictures of the people we'd lost. On my night I passed around half a dozen photographs and played a CD—songs that Matt had recorded with one of the bands he'd started in high school. I told myself I'd brought the CD because I wanted people to hear his music when they saw him. A deeper connection, something to make him more real. But I only played a few parts of a few tracks before skipping to the end: a live radio interview.

I stood at the head of the room next to the portable stereo, shifting my weight from leg to leg and looking out at the faces of the group. The pictures had already made the rounds, so everyone was staring at me. After Matt and his bandmates introduced themselves, I fast-forwarded the track until I heard my own barely recognizable nineteen-year-old voice, cracking through the speakers, through a cell phone, through six years.

I'd been driving to Birmingham that day with Ryan, who was my boyfriend then, and we'd heard Matt on the radio just as the signal had started to fade. I'd squealed with excitement and surprise and used Ryan's cell phone to call the station.

The recorded conversation began. A conversation not between my brother and me, but between the DJs and me. They asked me if I got sick of listening to Matt practice at home all the time, if he got into a lot of trouble, if he picked on me. They asked me how old I was. I told them he didn't play music at home nearly as much as he used to, and that he was smaller than I was, so I could kick his ass. Matt yelled in the background, "It's true!" and the DJs laughed. I told them I was nineteen, and they cued up canned applause to celebrate the fact that I was "legal." I wished the boys luck on their live performance and hung up.

And then came the part in the recording that I realized I'd been waiting for, the real reason I'd brought the CD. My heart beat faster, and my ears strained to hear the familiar words. A DJ asked my brother, "So, do you and your sister get along?"

And Matt said, "Yeah, we get along great!"

For a second I felt vindicated. *See?* I wanted to shout at all the faces smiling up at me, smiling because I was smiling at them. Grinning so hard my cheeks hurt. They nodded, commented on how lucky I was to have a recording of his voice, and my stomach dropped. My face went slack. I'd run into the brick wall that had blocked every effort to escape the black hole in the seven months since Matt's death—quitting my job, starting a new one, isolating myself, searching for someone exactly or nothing like me. My attempt to prove my brother's love to the group failed in the same way that everything else had: it didn't change what had happened.

I realized then that there was no clear, easy path through grief. What I really, truly, needed was impossible. I needed to turn back time, to erase my own mistakes to stop his. I needed not to grieve. I needed him not to be dead.

■■■■■■■■

Near the end of our meetings, a woman asked the facilitators how long it would be until she felt better. I remember the flood of understanding that came with her question, the voice in my head that pleaded with hers—*how long? How long until I find my way back to the life I had before he died? Until I can look at his face, see a boy who looks just like him on the other side of the street, without that vacuum forming in my chest? How long?*

I wanted, but did not expect, a concrete answer. I'd read several books about suicide and grief by then, and they had all said essentially the same thing—anything goes. There are no timelines, no rules, no standards. Everyone's experience of and reaction to a death is different, and there is no such thing as an invalid response. I figured the facilitators would feed us more of the same.

But there was no litany of platitudes and no hesitation. One facilitator, who'd lost her son roughly five years prior, immediately said, "Three years." She looked at the other facilitators, with raised eyebrows for confirmation. They did quick, silent calculations, shrugged, and nodded.

Three years. No matter how far away it seemed, I was relieved to have an end point. Exhausted by my search for the perfect path through grief, I told myself the only thing I could.

All you need is time.

hands

Questions had formed in the first days after Matt's death: why had he done it? What had pushed him over the edge? Why hadn't he told someone what he was feeling?

Why hadn't he told me?

I knew, even as the facilitator said three years, that waiting wouldn't be enough—I needed answers. And I was sure there were answers: in his blog, in the note, in the memories of my parents and his friends. But the thought of searching for them opened that black hole in my chest. Waiting would wear the vacuum down, I thought, make it possible for me to face the truth without falling apart.

The only problem was, in the meantime, I couldn't stop my mind from fabricating a story with the facts it did have—our twin attempts and the quote from *Night Falls Fast*. The story went like this:

Contagious aspect. I was first. I'll be next.

I thought about my brother every night while I lay awake in bed. Given our shared DNA and past histories, my own suicide seemed inevitable. It was out there, waiting for me—a land mine wired by genes and fears and grief. I imagined the urge would strike suddenly, as it had with my first attempt. I pictured myself doing the dishes, or riding a bicycle, or eating a slice of pizza, a voice inside me suddenly demanding that I die.

In the dark next to Ryan's sleeping body, I thought about my brother hanging in that doorway. I wondered what it felt like—what he'd felt. I pressed my hands to my throat until I gagged.

I suppose it goes without saying that I wasn't sleeping. I also hated to leave the house, couldn't stand to be around people, and constantly snapped at Ryan. I'd taken a job teaching at a local community college after I'd quit the library, but by January, three months before the first anniversary of Matt's death, I'd quit the teaching job, too. I was cracking under the weight of my grief. Not knowing what else to do, I made an appointment with my psychiatrist.

I'd been on antidepressants for over nine years by then, a span covering high school, college, and graduate school. There had been a year in the middle, around the time of my college graduation and wedding, when I'd tapered off the Paxil and experienced what I was told was the return of my original depression (and what I found out years later was a severe case of withdrawal). So, after Ryan and I moved to Chicago, I found a new psychiatrist and started taking Lexapro. By the start of 2004, I had finished grad school, gotten the library job, and purchased an apartment. I'd been symptom-free for a few years and was happily married. Ryan and I were talking about having children, and I was considering another shot at stopping the meds.

I'd never been comfortable with antidepressants. I'd spent developmental years—years when people establish personalities, discover who they are—on drugs that manipulated my brain chemistry. I constantly questioned whether my thoughts and feelings were actually mine, or whether they were the machinations of the chalky capsule that disintegrated in my stomach every morning. And just when I'd finally felt like my life was good enough, stable enough, to take a chance on the real me, Matt had died.

In the wake of my grief, my psychiatrist suggested supplementing my Lexapro with Wellbutrin. I'd tried it years before, when I'd tapered off the Paxil. It was supposed to ease the transition, but I'd begun crying uncontrollably after I took it, and had continued to do so on and off for the next two days, until I'd flushed the remaining twenty-seven tablets down the toilet. I told my psychiatrist I wasn't sure. He said to give it a try.

So I did—and I didn't cry. Within days I was full of energy, able to laugh and smile. But there was a problem, as there always seems to be with drugs that actually work. The first time I noticed it was during a photography class, while I was trying to cut a roll of negatives. I held the slick strip steady between the fingers of my left hand and raised the scissors with my right. As I brought the scissors to the edge of the negative and pressed them together, my hand jerked, slicing through the frame.

"Shit," I said, and I put down the scissors.

Thinking it was nerves, I made a fist and then relaxed my hand. I picked up the scissors again and took a deep breath, exhaling as I prepared to make the cut. It was no use. My hands shook so badly that I could barely see what I was doing.

Matt's hands started shaking when he was about fifteen. Tremors are a possible side effect of nearly every medication used to treat bipolar disorder, and he was on so many pills (every morning Mom set a half-full Dixie cup of them on the kitchen counter and he knocked it back as fast as a shot of tequila—without water) that there was no way to divine the culprit.

There are plenty of other unpleasant side effects caused by the medications used to treat bipolar disorder and depression. Matt and I didn't talk about it, so I didn't know if he was feeling tired or dizzy, had constipation, muscle weakness, nausea, indigestion, diarrhea, ataxia, headaches, insomnia, anxiety, or blurred vision. But I saw his hands every day. Holding a fork or a pen, paused in the air midgesture or hanging at his sides, his fingers trembled like the last leaves in autumn wind. Their tips were bulbous, swollen around the chewed-down fingernails. I chewed my fingernails, too, and they had the same red and ragged look. At any time, either one of us could be seen wincing, finger in mouth, a small tear of skin tugged off between teeth, sucking at the resulting stream of hot blood.

We both had our father's hands, delicate and thin. The knobs of our knuckles and small wrists jutted out. When our fingers moved, the fan of tendons on the backs of our hands popped and shifted under our skin like the levers of a manual typewriter. By the time Matt was diagnosed as bipolar, his hands were larger than mine. His shuddering fingers were still slender, but they had grown long. The blond down on his forearms had been replaced by darker hair that would, in a few years, thicken and spread until it filled in the curve of fuzz that stopped just below the knuckles of his pinkies.

After a while he took control of the tremors, made them his own, constantly drumming on any available surface: the kitchen table, the countertop, his bare white chest with its tiny patch of twisted black hairs. He hammered out a beat, his head joining in with a steady bounce, eyebrows raised, a crooked smile. Sometimes a hum would echo the music that played in his head.

Matt's hands were how I knew he was really dead. At the wake he looked like he was sleeping, or passed out drunk. His hair was long, like it had been in junior high, when he'd parted it down the middle and tucked it behind his ears. The body's resemblance to my living brother was so unnerving that I concentrated on his chest, watched for movement just in case. Just in case they'd made a mistake, hadn't noticed that he wasn't dead while they drained out all his blood and pumped him full of embalming fluid. But then my eyes wandered down to his stomach and I knew. There was no mistake. His hands, a younger, larger version of my own, were rigid. Completely still.

I stared at them. Forced together atop his stomach, his thin fingers were as curled as dried bird claws, as if he'd been holding on so tightly, for so long, that they would never fully release. The skin was caked with makeup—even his chewed-down fingernails—the granules of powder visible in every fold. An attempt to disguise the discoloration that, I assumed, had been caused by blood pooling throughout the nearly full day that had passed before someone had found him. My brother had used gravity to exit the world, and gravity had left its stain.

My parents told me later that the full autopsy report revealed there had been no drugs in his system. None. Which meant he'd stopped taking his medication at least two weeks before his death. The real him. I understood.

———

I took the Wellbutrin for a few weeks that winter before the first anniversary of Matt's death, and in the pauses between typing emails or brushing my hair or changing the channel, I looked down and saw my brother's shaking hands.

I didn't tell my psychiatrist. Just like I didn't tell him about the land mine, or the times I'd gripped my throat. I didn't tell him how once upon a time my brother's and my being the same had meant that we would both be okay.

I told him that the Wellbutrin wasn't worth it, but I didn't tell him it wasn't because of my shaking hands. I think part of me knew, even then, that I was using it to cover up something I needed to feel—even though I wasn't quite sure why I needed to feel it. I went back to taking just the Lexapro. Back to the standoff with my brother's untold story. I went back to waiting.

one year

April 30, 2005. The first anniversary. Because it was a Saturday, my parents flew from Alabama to Michigan, and my husband and I drove from Chicago to Michigan, so we could . . . there is no good word for what we did. According to my thesaurus, the antonyms of *celebrate* are *disregard, ignore, neglect,* and *forget*—the vocabulary of my survival tactic of avoidance, what I would have asked to do if I'd thought it was possible.

Instead we regarded, acknowledged, remembered. Relived. We went to the church where we'd held Matt's funeral service and sat through a Mass said in his honor. We caravanned to the cemetery and stood at the foot of his grave, sipped cans of Pabst Blue Ribbon (his favorite beer), and ate handfuls of Cheez-Its (his favorite snack). My mother cried, dabbed at her eyes with wadded-up tissues from her purse. My father rocked back on his heels and exhaled through his nose. Ryan stood quietly. I shifted from foot to foot and wondered how long we were going to stand there. As children, Matt and I had been to that cemetery dozens of times to visit the grave of our grandmother, who'd died when our father was only three years old. All we'd known of her was a single black-and-white photograph. All we'd known of death was a few goldfish and two hamsters. So every Christmas and Mother's Day we watched our parents look at the ground for a few minutes, and then wandered off to search for headstones with the strange insignia of the Masons, or nineteenth-century born-on dates.

As I fidgeted on the damp spring grass of Matt's grave, I fought that old urge to wander. I should have been crying, I thought. I should have been thinking of him. I suppose I was. I was thinking of the blond-haired boy who'd picked through markers beside me all those years ago—a lifetime, it seemed. Another life. A life that no longer felt real.

In the year since his death, our past had dislodged itself from my present. For as long as I could remember, I'd seen the timeline of my life laid out in my mind: a path curving up through the early years, cutting straight through elementary school, turning a bend in middle school, angling steeply through high school, and arcing gently over eight or nine decades toward who knew what. I'd always seen him on that same line, following me, a few paces behind. After he died, I felt like I'd jumped the track. I was on an identical line, but it wasn't the same. On this new path I had the feeling—against all logic, evidence, and memory—that he'd never existed. He was still on the old path, the one we'd shared.

I'd tried explaining this to my therapist. He'd looked at me like I was nuts. I didn't blame him—it sounded nuts. But I didn't know how else to describe it. I knew what was real, that I'd had a brother and that what was left of him was in a box beneath my feet. But what I knew couldn't touch what I felt.

I stared down at his headstone, a rectangle of granite sunk into sod, carved with a border, his name, the dates of his birth and death. BELOVED, it said beneath that. SON. BROTHER. FRIEND. And lower still: MY MOTHER IS A FISH. Something for future generations of children to stumble upon and wonder over.

I'd encountered that sentence for the first time when I'd read William Faulkner's *As I Lay Dying* during my sophomore year in college. A chapter in itself, the line is the thought of Vardaman, a child who sees the light leave his mother's eyes and trips between "is" and "was." Here and gone. A child who remembers the dirt-coated eye of a fish he caught, split, gutted, scaled, and cut into pieces. *Not-fish now,* he thinks, *not-blood.* And then the connection, the understanding of his mother's death perfectly distilled in that single sentence—"My mother is a fish."

When I returned home from class that day, Matt was in the kitchen. I pulled out my book and showed him.

"It's the shortest chapter in literary history," I said, and he turned the phrase in his mouth like a jewel and smiled.

Engraving it on the headstone had been Mom's idea. Matt had used the quote to personalize his Amazon.com profile, to differentiate himself from the dozens of other people who shared his name.

"It was how I could find his Wish List," Mom had explained to the saleswoman at the monument company, who hadn't actually seemed to need an explanation. In fact, she'd laughed. We'd all laughed, the mood in that office a sudden shift from the earlier solemnity of dropping Matt's suit off at the funeral home and buying the cemetery plots. Was it the warm smile of the saleswoman? The knowledge that we were almost done for the day? The fact that, finally, we were dealing with something besides his body, the granite rectangle a welcome symbol of distance, the first sign of breathing room? Or was it the quote itself, Mom's ability to salvage something tender from that early wreckage, reminding us that it hadn't been so long since he'd been part of a crowd, and had needed differentiation?

Regardless of the reason, one year later, the grief as settled as the flat earth around his stone, we couldn't seem to summon any of that relief. I listened to my mother cry, watched my father rock, sensed my husband waiting at the edges of our mourning. I thought about our fractured timelines, how purchasing the headstone was one of the first memories on my solo track.

And then the whine of bagpipes broke the silence of the cemetery. Mom stopped crying, and all four of us turned our heads. We saw a lone piper dressed in a kilt, standing at a grave on the other side of the drive.

A fragment of memory floated to the surface of my mind. My brother's voice. Our last conversation. *Maybe you should learn to play the bagpipes*, Matt had said. I wanted to laugh. I didn't, but I smiled. All of us smiled. A collective exhalation, like the shift in the office of the monument company. Timing so perfect I was tempted to call it something more than a coincidence. Pity, maybe, from the universe. Or maybe beneath the weight of such absurdity we broke through that thin plane between humor and pain. Matt's death, my splintered timeline, the context-less quote, the bagpipe serenade, the stretch of unbroken ground to the left of his grave that the rest of us were crawling closer to with every second—heartbreaking, incomprehensible, and utterly ridiculous.

One year. A milestone. And there I was, smiling at my brother's graveside. I thought we had survived the worst, that with each day, each month, each year, our grief would lessen. I was sure that the lightness of the moment was a taste of the very near future.

I was wrong.

I don't remember how long we stayed and listened to the music. What, if anything, we said. How long that lightness lasted, and what it felt like when it slipped away.

second chance

I thought I would know when I was ready to look for answers. I also thought being ready meant everything would be easy. And though I'd convinced myself that I was waiting, that I wasn't capable of facing any part of Matt's past, I renewed my friendship with Tim—one of the first friends my brother had made after we moved to Alabama.

After the move, Matt and I were the sole sense of familiarity and safety left in each other's lives. We became, for a while, close in the way we had been as children. Alone together, again, we spent hours playing video games, listening to CDs, or watching MTV and *Mystery Science Theater 3000*.

Because we were "Yankees," in addition to being new kids, the friends-making process was slow. The few friends we did make in those early months we shared, and Tim was one of them. I hung out with Tim a lot, more than any of Matt's other friends. I crashed their jam sessions and horned in on Sega Genesis marathons. When the three of us were together, we most often listened to music—shutting the blinds and turning off the lights in Matt's room so we could dance in the pulse of a strobe light.

By the time I finished high school, Matt and I had carved out separate social lives; we no longer needed each other as we once had. I'd started college, moved out of the house. We had new friends and new interests. Matt and Tim still traveled in the same circles, but I didn't see him at the house anymore. I didn't see him anywhere anymore. In fact, I'd forgotten all about him—until the memorial service we had at my parents' church in Alabama.

The service was well attended, to say the least. Ryan and I had gotten married in that church, so I knew that it sat three hundred people. Our wedding had filled two-thirds of the pews. Matt's memorial service was standing room only. Rows packed with my parents' friends and coworkers, fellow parishioners, and a few dozen of Matt's friends.

Afterward the priest asked everyone to stay for coffee and donuts, which would be served in the rec hall. The hall was a large building next to the church, the two doorways joined by a short stretch of sidewalk. Since my parents, Ryan, and I were the first to leave the church, we were the first to arrive at the hall. The door was propped open, and the light from inside spilled halfway across the sidewalk, dwindling into darkness before it reached the church.

Once we entered the hall and turned around, we saw that a line had already formed. Our intention was for everyone to come in straightaway, have a seat in one of the hundreds of folding chairs at one of the dozens of folding tables, and let us make the rounds. But somehow we ended up pinned at the door, greeting each guest like a receiving line at a wedding.

After fifteen or twenty minutes, the heels of my feet were sore, the backs of my knees stiff. When I looked out the door of the hall, I saw a sea of shadowed faces ebbing into silhouettes—no end in sight. One by one people told me how they knew my parents or my brother, and how sorry they were for my loss. And then a woman stood in front of me with open arms. She had wavy, shoulder-length brown hair and a thin face. Her eyes were large and turned down at the corners. She looked familiar, but I couldn't place her. I didn't realize it was Lorraine until I saw who hovered behind her—her son, Tim.

When I'd first met him, almost ten years before, Tim had been short, with a head of thick brown hair, a quiet voice, and a deferential demeanor. He'd been gentle, laid back. I'd had no idea that Tim was bipolar until after we'd found out my brother was, when Mom had started talking about it with Lorraine. Tim had been diagnosed in childhood, several years before Matt had.

Lorraine hugged me and then stepped aside, leaving Tim standing in front of me. His head was shaved almost to the skin. He was nearly a foot taller than I was, thin wrists sticking out from the sleeves of a gray flannel shirt. He wore black slacks and black shoes, and his eyes were bright green behind wire-rimmed glasses. It felt strange to be happy to see someone in such a circumstance, but I was. Tim was a connection to my brother and our past. He brought me back to the last time I felt like I really knew Matt, the last time I felt like Matt and I really knew each other. Tim smiled nervously, his eyes resting on mine for a second, before darting down, side to side, down, side to side.

"Oh my God! I can't believe you're here. It's so good to see you," I said, pulling him in for a hug. He felt like bones in my arms. I asked him to write down his email address for me. I hugged a few more people, and then Tim reached through the line to hand me a scrap of paper. I gave him a nod and he gave me a wave. After he left, I thought about how he and Matt had grown apart, how Matt and I had grown apart, how we had all changed. How much of my brother's life I had missed in the process of our separate struggles to push into adulthood. And then a strange thought surfaced. Maybe I could be there for Tim like I hadn't been for Matt. I saw a surrogate baby brother. A second chance.

———

By the first anniversary of Matt's death, Tim and I were corresponding frequently enough that I was getting a glimpse into his life—a bipolar life. I still didn't know much about bipolar disorder, still doubted Matt's diagnosis, but I was also wary of the last two years of Matt's life, the years we'd drifted furthest apart. I looked to Tim to show me what I'd missed.

Typically he wrote to me about four things: his struggle to keep a job, his inability to hold on to a car (the combination of his medication and heavy drinking resulted in lots of accidents), his romantic entanglements, and his music. If Tim was depressed, he couldn't get a job without a car and couldn't get a car without a job, and that made him feel like a loser. If Tim wasn't depressed, then job prospects were listed, money for a car was being saved, a new band was being formed, and he was seeing a new, amazing girl. We wrote back and forth a lot about the depression. I urged him to see a therapist, which he refused to do. He called me on the phone occasionally, either manic or drunk or both, and our conversations were rarely less than two hours long. He would chatter excitedly about books, art, music. Ryan would poke his head around the corner of the stairs every now and then and raise his eyebrows, and I'd shrug. He'd whisper, "Who are you talking to?" I'd mouth *Tim* and he would say, "Ooooh," while nodding his head. I was okay with the nature of our relationship for a while, until the fall of 2005, six months after the first anniversary of Matt's death.

It was the third week of October, and Ryan and I were back in Tuscaloosa to visit my parents and go to a University of Alabama football game. I had promised Tim I would call him so we could get together while I was in town, but every day I put it off. I rationalized that it wasn't anything personal; I was busy visiting with my parents. Really, the week just slid by. I hadn't even noticed how quickly. It absolutely wasn't intentional.

Except it was. Tim had been in a downward spiral the previous few weeks. He'd sent me several rambling emails and had called me late one night, drunk, to talk about how depressed he was. His most recent girlfriend, Ashley, was pregnant, and he was freaking out. He didn't have a job or a car. I told him not to worry, that everything would be okay. They would figure things out together. Maybe having a child could be the best thing that had ever happened to him. He seemed to relax after that. He sent me an email the next day that said he was excited about it, confident that he could make it work. Still, the discomfort his phone call and emails caused remained a heavy pit in my stomach.

By Friday night, the end of our weeklong visit in Tuscaloosa, the guilt caught up with me and I knew I had to call Tim. The best I could hope for, I thought, was to control the circumstances of our meeting. I planned to invite him to lunch the next day. Since my parents, my husband, and I were going to the football game in the afternoon, I figured we could meet on campus. The rest of my family would be around to keep Tim from getting too emotional, and the game would put a time limit on our visit. It was the perfect plan.

I took the portable phone from the kitchen into my parents'

bedroom, dialed Tim's number, and paced as the phone rang, my lower lip pinched between my teeth. Voicemail. I exhaled and released my lip. I left Tim a message, apologizing that it had taken me so long to contact him and asking him if he wanted to meet for lunch, but before I could even hang up the phone, another call came through—Tim's number on the caller ID.

"Hey!" I answered.

"Hey . . . Kelley? Is that you?" His voice was faint beneath thumping bass, shouts, shrieks, and laughter. It was also thick and slow. I figured he was drunk.

"Yeah. Where are you?"

"Finn's," he said. A new bar downtown, one of the dozen that had mushroomed after I graduated and moved away.

"Oh, okay. Did you get my voicemail?" I asked.

"What?"

"My voicemail," I said a little more loudly, cupping my hand around the mouthpiece of the phone. "I wanted to know if you want to go to lunch tomorrow before the game."

A cacophony of bar noise poured into my ear.

"Tim?"

More noise. Had he passed out?

"Tim!"

"Yeah . . . hey . . . what's up?"

I laughed nervously. "Are you drunk or what?"

"No . . . I haven't . . . had any . . . drinks. . . . It's . . . these . . . pills. . . ."

My stomach dropped. "Tim"—my voice grew louder—"what pills? What pills did you take?"

"All . . . all of 'em. . . ."

My heart began to pound in my throat, and the phone shook in the tightness of my grip, bumping against my ear.

"Tim? Tim! TIM!" I screamed. Nothing. "TIM! WAKE UP—DO YOU HEAR ME? WAKE UP!"

Oh shit, what do I do? Do I hang up? Do I call 911? Do I call the bar? I pressed the phone into my ear as hard as I could, straining for any sound. After a few seconds, I heard faint, faraway voices. "Dude, are you okay?" one said. "Is he okay?" said another. "I think this guy passed out or something," said a third.

"HELLO! HELLO, PLEASE, CAN YOU HEAR ME!" I screamed into the receiver. "PICK UP THE PHONE! HE TOOK PILLS; HE NEEDS HELP! HELLO!"

Click.

The silence entered my ear and filled my brain. Seconds passed as I waited, not thinking, not speaking, not believing—frozen. Another *click* and a dial tone broke the silence.

My fingers trembled as I pressed the buttons: 9-1-1.

———

I explained the situation to the emergency operator, who assured me that the paramedics were on their way to the bar. My mother called Lorraine to let her know what was happening. But I couldn't sit in the silence of our house, waiting to find out if Tim would survive. My father and I got in the car and sped toward downtown.

I saw the flashing red lights as soon as we turned onto Twenty-Third Avenue, and I jumped out of the car after we pulled up to the back of the ambulance. I caught a glimpse of Tim before the paramedics closed the doors: a series of lumps beneath a white sheet. He wasn't moving. I stepped toward the ambulance, and a police officer stopped me.

"Hold on, now—you can't go over there."

"That's my friend in there. I'm the one who called 911."

"Well, let's let the paramedics do their job."

"Is he alive?"

"Yes, he's alive."

"Is he going to be okay?"

"I don't know, but they been sittin' here for a while now, so I think that's a good sign. If he was in trouble, you know, they woulda been gone fast."

Tim's parents pulled up just as the ambulance left. Lorraine sprang from the car and started firing questions at the officer I'd been speaking to.

The police officer was gentle, answering her questions and reassuring her as much as he could. After he left, I asked her if she wanted us to go to the hospital with her, but she said no, we should go home and get some rest.

"We'll call you in the morning to see how he's doing," I said. Then I added, "You call us if you need anything," because it seemed like the kind of thing you should say in a crisis. She wrapped her arms around me and whispered into my ear.

"Thank you."

In the morning, Mom called Lorraine to see how Tim was doing. If he was all right, we would go to the game. If not, I didn't know. But Lorraine said he was going to make it. He was in intensive care, and we could come and visit him if we wanted. Only two people at a time.

Lorraine was waiting for us when we got there. "You saved his life," she said as she embraced me.

I didn't know what to say.

She gave us the pass to go see him. He was sleeping, but the nurse told us to go ahead and wake him up. From the doorway he looked the same as he had the night before: lumps under a sheet. When I got closer, I could see that the pale skin of his inner arms was exposed and his head drooped. My mother went to the left side of the bed, I went right. She put her hand on his head, and a tear slid down her cheek. I thought about Matt's wake, how I'd wanted to place my hand on his head just like that, how the stiffness of his hair had stopped me. I'd touched his shoulder instead and felt nothing but the padding of his suit.

Tim's eyelids opened a sliver. "Hey . . . Mrs. Schwartz? What are you doing here?" A smile spread across his face.

"We came to see you," I said, and his heavy-lidded eyes turned to me.

"Wow . . . that's great . . . you didn't have to do that." His speech was slow, tangled.

"As if we wouldn't come!" I forced the corners of my mouth up. I put my hand on his shoulder, felt the knob of bone and the warmth of his skin through the gown.

"Wow . . . that's so great . . . thanks. You know . . . I'm really sorry."

"It's okay, Tim. You're going to be okay," my mom said, picking up his hand and squeezing it.

"Thank . . . you . . . guys. . . . I'm . . . so . . . sorry . . ." Tim's eyelids sagged.

"We'll let you get some sleep now," I said, leaning in and stretching my right arm across his neck to his left shoulder—the closest I could get to a hug.

Back in the waiting room, Lorraine explained everything to us. The night before, Tim was supposed to meet his girlfriend's parents for the first time. Ashley's father was a minister, and none too thrilled about his daughter's "situation." They were going to meet at a restaurant next door to the bar. On his way downtown, Tim stopped at the drugstore and picked up his prescriptions, along with a six-pack of beer. In the parking lot, he drank the beer and swallowed all four bottles of his medication. The alcohol and pills kicked in fast. While he was on the phone with me, he wandered out from the bar to the sidewalk in front of the restaurant. That was where he passed out. Bystanders called the police, thinking that he was merely drunk. I had done for Tim what I hadn't been able to do for my brother: I had saved his life.

And yet—in the wake of that gift, that miracle, that second chance—not a damn thing changed.

two years

April 30, 2006. The second anniversary. A beautiful spring day, warm and blue-skied. Once again Ryan and I met up with my parents in Michigan. Once again we sat through a Mass in the church where we'd had Matt's funeral. Once again we drove to the cemetery and stood at my brother's grave. My father pulled the cans of PBR out of a paper bag, and there was a collective hiss and pop when we cracked them open. He stuffed the rolled-up bag under his arm and passed me the Cheez-Its. I wanted to remember something when I dug my hand into the box. Wanted the cardboard rumble of shifting crackers or the sharp smell of powdered cheddar to trigger my brother's face, his laugh, his life. But I was stuck in the present, feet rooted firmly to the earth, crushing the thin, pale blades of reborn grass.

As usual, Mom started to cry. We'd gone to the cemetery alone together the previous summer, the only visit with no husbands, no beer, no Cheez-Its. But her tears couldn't be left behind. As they'd fallen, she'd thanked me.

"It's so good to be able to cry with someone and not feel bad about it. I know that all my crying is hard on your father."

"Of course you can cry with me—cry anytime you want," I'd said as I'd taken her hand. I'd wanted to mean it, so I hadn't told her the truth: the more she cried, the harder I became. The harder I pushed down my pain to be strong for her because she'd always been so strong for us. She'd never complained. Not about laundry or dishes, dinner or carpools, leaving her entire family to move across the country to a state she'd never been to, or the breakdowns, pills, rehab, and hospitalizations that followed. During our still-daily telephone conversations, she said things like, "I'd do it all over again, even if I knew how it would turn out. I wouldn't trade a single second." And, "Sometimes when I'm thinking about him, I feel his presence and I know he's right there with me."

If I had the choice, I thought, *I would rather have been an only child.* And when I thought about him, closed my eyes and searched in the dark for the glimmer of his soul, I felt nothing.

I hated myself for thinking it. Hated her for not thinking it. Hated her for making me hate her. Hated myself for hating her. Hated my brother for making me hate everything.

But at the cemetery my anger was buried under numbness. I wanted to want to throw the beer and the Cheez-Its, to beat my fists into the ground, to scream, to cry, to get it all out of me. But all I really wanted to do was leave.

My mother cried beside me, my father rocked back on his heels, my husband stood quietly. A few dozen yards away there was another family, a mother and father with a smattering of little children and a massive bouquet of balloons. Their voices carried on the breeze:

"Say 'happy birthday, Grandma'!" the mother said.

"Happy birfday, Gama!" echoed a tiny chorus, and two dozen ribbon-tailed pastel orbs bobbed into the clear blue sky.

I bet Gama didn't hang herself.

———

After the facilitator mentioned the three-year mark, I imagined that my grief would ease steadily, slip away bit by bit each day. I was confused, at two years, to find that it hadn't. If anything, it had gotten worse.

There's this thing about denial—it doesn't work. I'd tried to avoid Matt's death whenever I could, and when I hadn't been able to, I'd tried to separate my thoughts and fears and feelings, bury them deep inside me, confine them to the pages of my journal or the office of my therapist. It was what I had to do in order to get up every morning, take a shower, walk the dog. Go to the part-time job I'd taken at a gym, buy groceries, wash clothes. The private space I'd made for my grief was the only thing that kept me living—but I was running out of room.

Ryan, being closest to me in proximity, bore the brunt of my rising anxiety. "I can't take this shit anymore!" I'd scream at him in response to a misplaced dish, and, "You never fucking listen to me; you don't even care about me!" when he forgot to pick up the dry cleaning. I threw countless CDs, pens, and books. I shattered my cell phone. I bruised the side of my palm repeatedly by pounding on the inside of the car door, the back of the couch, assorted doorjambs and walls. One night I nearly broke a knuckle punching our granite countertop. But none of it was enough. I'd rage for hours over trivial inconveniences, stomping up and down the hallway, slamming doors, seeking layer upon layer of pain—physical, mental, directed at myself, directed at my husband, directed at the world—until I melted into tears. But even then I screamed, "GET AWAY FROM ME" when my husband reached out his hand. I'd lock myself in the bathroom and lie on the cold floor in the dark, my cheek pressed into the tile, until the tears stopped and a sickening stone of shame formed in my stomach. I would go to Ryan then, my red and ruined face bent down, and beg for his forgiveness.

"I'm sorry I overreacted," I'd say. "I don't know what's wrong with me." Which was a lie. I did know, but I couldn't say it. I didn't think I was allowed to say it. It had been two years—I was supposed to be getting better, not worse. And even if I'd felt like I could say it, I wouldn't have known how. *I'm sorry I yelled at you—my brother is dead.*

Of course Ryan knew, too. He never yelled back at me during my breakdowns. He always accepted my apologies, hugged me and stroked my hair. I attributed this to his patience, his easygoing manner, and my good fortune. When I ask him about it now, how he managed to stand there while I screamed at him, why he let me be so mean, he shakes his head.

"You weren't mean," he says. "You were sad."

I was sad and beyond, caught somewhere between despair, rage, and panic—territory all too familiar. It was exactly what I'd felt as a teenager stuck in Alabama, equal parts helpless and pissed. Back then Matt and I had been there for each other. Back then we'd had our parents to blame. We'd known we wouldn't stay there forever. We'd swallowed our pills and counted the days, and then we'd left.

This time I was alone. This time it was Matt's fault. And I was stuck in this new world, this world without him, for the rest of my life.

As I stood by Matt's grave on the second anniversary, watched the balloons the other family had released rise, shrink down to pin-size dots, and vanish, I realized that time wouldn't erode my fear or guilt. In order to get better, to feel good enough to delve into the words my brother left behind, the answers, I needed a release.

And yet I failed to recognize my bouts of misdirected anger as necessary ruptures in the wall around my grief. I wanted my grief to rise up out of my heart, my head, and disappear into the sky like balloons—not break open inside me and bleed into the lives of the people I loved. I was determined to clutch my grief even tighter then, to close in on myself even more. The safest thing to do, the only thing to do, was go to the cemetery without anyone else. Face the solid, grass-covered fact of my brother's death alone.

Over the next few weeks, I fantasized about the trip. I'd go over a weekend so that Ryan could stay home with our dog. I would drive, stay in a hotel, tell no one. I would bring a blanket to sit on and maybe a stereo, with some of Matt's music, or at least some of his favorite music. I would talk to him like he was right there with me, like people do in the movies. And I would *feel* him, the way Mom did.

But every time I thought about it—not fantasized, thought—five hours in the car *alone*, a night in a crappy hotel *alone*, another five hours in the car *alone*, my heart started to pound. At the time it didn't seem necessary to question my reaction. It was easier to decide I didn't need to make a special trip. I just had to find a way to get to the cemetery by myself the next time I was in town. Just before the second anniversary, my parents had left Alabama, packed up, and moved back to Michigan. They'd done it to be closer to my mother's parents and my father's siblings, closer to Ryan and me, closer to Matt's grave. I could visit the cemetery over Thanksgiving. *Just six more months*, I told myself, *and then everything will be fine.*

the real me

Around the second anniversary, when my grief was lunging and gnashing like a caged animal, when I burned with the effort of trying to hold all my feelings in, I decided to stop taking antidepressants. My official reason was that Ryan and I wanted to have children, and new data was coming out about the link between birth defects and SSRIs. So I was telling the truth: I didn't want to play the odds.

But I wasn't telling the whole truth. My brother had ended his life unmedicated—the real him, I'd thought. Sick of the constant fear that I would follow suit, I decided it was time to meet the real me.

A friend of mine once described her experience on Lexapro as dampening the reverb of her emotions. It didn't keep her from feeling, she said. It just kept her feelings from echoing, from reaching into situations and relationships where they didn't belong. She also said that the medication didn't make her feel any less like herself.

This sounded like a perfect description of how the meds were supposed to work. The problem was that, even though I took the same drug, I had no idea what she was talking about. I'd been on some form of psychotropic medication since I was sixteen years old. By the time I decided to stop taking meds, I was twenty-seven. I'd been medicated for nearly half my life. I didn't know who I was without them.

More important, I didn't know if that person could survive. Did suicide lurk in my core? My brother went off the meds to die. I was going off the meds to see if I could live.

I'd already tried to come off antidepressants once—the summer before Ryan and I got married, which also happened to be the summer before my senior year of college. When I'd first started SSRIs, my doctor had said I'd only need to take them for a year or two. By the time Ryan and I got engaged and moved into an off-campus apartment together, I'd been on them for four. Life was good, I was fine, so I figured maybe I didn't need them anymore. I brought it up with my psychiatrist and she supported the idea, but suggested that I taper my dosage down slowly because there was a risk of withdrawal—namely nausea, blurred vision, and a general feeling of "mild discomfort." Which is all I experienced. At first. But after a few months on my new, lower dosage, I was walking a tightrope of agitation, irritation, and rage. Nights were the worst. I lay awake in bed, listening to Ryan breathe, the rhythm of his gentle wheeze like water torture. Every rise and fall of his chest grated the underside of my skin, tightened the giant fist that gripped my heart and lungs and made me dig my fingernails into my palms. I held it back as long as I could, thinking, hoping, praying that somehow, if I waited long enough, it would release me. That if I kept very still it wouldn't squeeze tears from my eyes, wouldn't tear screams from my throat, wouldn't clutch and strangle for hours and leave me limp on the floor, a quivering puddle of hot, wet salt and snot, exhaustion and shame. But it always did. Usually around 3:00 a.m.

By the end of that semester, it was my nightly routine: fall into bed exhausted by 10:00 p.m.; lie awake, staring at the ceiling, trying to slow my spinning thoughts until my eyes were dry and sticky at 3:00 a.m., have a panic attack and cry in Ryan's arms until 4:00 a.m.; fall into a shallow sleep on the futon in the spare bedroom until 7:00 a.m.; get up, go to class, and try to pretend like I was a normal person.

One night a few weeks before finals, as I shrieked and shook during my regularly scheduled 3:00 a.m. panic attack, someone pounded on our front door. It was the police. The people who lived above us had called them. An officer came into our bedroom and crouched beside me. I couldn't stop crying.

"Did he hurt you?" he asked. I shook my head. "You can tell me if he did. I promise everything will be okay." I shook my head again, starting to cry even harder.

"What's wrong?" He put a hand on my arm. I couldn't answer. "Please, you have to tell me. I can't leave until you tell me."

"You're not going to believe me," I sobbed.

"It's okay—just tell me."

It wasn't okay. I didn't want to tell him. I knew it sounded ridiculous. He wouldn't understand. I didn't understand. But I said it anyway, because there wasn't anything else to say.

"I can't sleep."

They left. There must have been further discussion, talk of doctors or herbal tea, skeptical glances at Ryan, but I don't remember any of that. I remember the next morning, when the confusion, frustration, and humiliation settled like a weight on my chest. And I remember a few weeks later, when we moved.

My psychiatrist tried to tell me it was the return of my original depression. I disagreed. I didn't know what it was, but I knew it was different. Worse. Still, I was determined to quit the meds and refused to go back to my regular dosage. The panic attacks, the insomnia, the agitation, the crying—I was afraid that if I caved, I would be admitting that that was the real me.

By the time I hit the one-year mark (still on a small, but stubborn, dose of medication), I was sleeping two hours a night and shitting blood. I'd lost twenty pounds. My parents threatened to have me hospitalized. I managed to convince them it was just stress. I swore I'd be fine once the summer was over. By September I had graduated, gotten married, and moved to Chicago, where it took a new psychiatrist, a new antidepressant, and six months of lying on the couch watching daytime television to right myself.

I surrendered. Maybe I was just one of those people. Maybe I would always have to be on medication. There was no shame in it, everyone assured me—but I wasn't assured. I felt weak. I felt like a failure. I was years away from understanding that no one gets through life without help, and that it comes to us in different forms at different times.

But part of me was also resolute. I didn't know why or how or when, but I knew I would find a way to live without the pills. I knew that there was someone under all the layers of chemicals.

I never dreamed what it would take to meet her.

When I decided to go off the antidepressants the second time, two years after Matt's death, I spoke to my psychiatrist about the problems I'd had during my first try. He mentioned withdrawal but was skeptical about my level of symptoms. Maybe I had just tried coming off too quickly? Maybe it was the particular drug I'd been on? Paxil was known to be more difficult to stop than other medications. He didn't think I'd have the same reaction this time.

I started the same way I had before: with a gradual step-down in dosage. Nothing happened at first, and I was elated. My doctor was right! Everything would be okay. But then, after a few months, once I got down to the lowest possible dosage, I started having dizzy spells and nausea.

"It's normal," my doctor said. "We can push through it. It won't last."

He was right—it didn't last. The dizziness and nausea faded into crawling skin and insomnia. My body buzzed with electric sensations so disturbing I scratched at myself until I bled. Every time I closed my eyes, I felt like I was standing at the edge of a bottomless pit and leaning forward, with nothing to stop me falling. I thought about my brother and how he'd quit his medication. Was this what he had felt? If so, I could understand why he'd ended his life. Because during my first full week without the Lexapro—between sobs, with vertigo so severe I couldn't stand up, so desperate and sick I couldn't stop pounding my head against the wall—I threatened to do the same. Ryan called my psychiatrist, picked up an emergency prescription for Xanax, and held my hand until I fell into a restless sleep.

Nowadays they have a term for this: SSRI discontinuation syndrome. The range of symptoms varies from the common, mild symptoms that my first psychiatrist was aware of to reactions as severe as mine. It's difficult to pin down numbers. One website says one out of every five people taking SSRIs will experience moderate to severe withdrawal if they cease taking them. Another says 25 percent. Yet another says 20. One says 35–78 percent of people who reduce their dosage of SSRIs by ten-milligram increments or more, after at least five weeks of treatment, will develop at least one symptom of discontinuation syndrome. Most websites mention that a small number of patients experience extreme or intolerable symptoms when stopping their antidepressants.

How small is small? When I sat across from my psychiatrist at our next appointment, he looked at me incredulously, as if he couldn't believe that a one-fourth reduction in my dosage had had such powerful consequences.

"It's very rare," he said.

"How rare?" I asked.

"One in a thousand, maybe?"

According to an article in *USA Today,* twenty-seven million Americans were taking antidepressants in 2005. Drop three zeros off that figure and you've got enough people to found a midsize city—picket fences, an old-timey downtown, a couple of diners, a library, a hospital, a community swimming pool, a bank, a decent school system—but you wouldn't want to live there, because if the pharmacy ran dry all the residents would be crying, screaming, banging their heads into walls, puking, and clawing at their skin. Welcome to Eli Lillyville.

There are a few options for Eli Lillyvillians. One is to get back on the medication and stay on it. Another is to white-knuckle your way through the pain. The third option, the one that worked for me, is to go on Prozac and start the step-down process all over again. Prozac has a longer half-life than any other SSRI, which means that it lingers in the body long enough to keep withdrawal symptoms at bay.

I tapered off the Prozac just like I'd tapered off the Lexapro, shaving down to micromilligrams and stretching out my doses over days, then weeks, even months. The withdrawal symptoms settled into what felt like a familiar film of depression. In the meantime, unable to do much of anything in the face of that film, I quit my job at the gym. I focused all my energy on survival. A small part of me was buoyed by the knowledge that my symptoms were chemically induced. They were not the real me. But I was still going to have to get through them.

In all, from my first Lexapro reduction to the last sliver of Prozac I swallowed, the process took about two years. I wanted there to be a moment when something shifted, like a cloud passing to reveal a brilliant ray of sun. I wanted to know, intuitively, that I had become "myself." Of course that didn't happen. What happened instead was that I spent a lot of time waiting. I wrote. I grieved. Ryan and I went on trips to Jamaica and San Francisco. I met new people and made new friends. I meditated. I ran. I cooked and cleaned and did the laundry. And little by little I began to see that I was doing it: I was living. And I was doing it without drugs. I cried more—but I laughed more, too. I had a lot more orgasms. I also had more anxiety. I felt raw and stripped but full of joy and wonder. The margins of my experience had stretched to new limits, and I spent years cautiously exploring the borderlands.

Eventually I started to understand that those margins aren't me, either. It took a life-threatening illness, a couple of surgeries, the loss of a pregnancy, and a return to SSRIs for me to conclude that there is a light at my core that has nothing to do with my mind, my fears, or my feelings. The real me is the same person as the real everyone else: the stillness and love that we all have at our center.

My brother had the stillness, too, though he didn't believe it. He'd be rolling his eyes right now at this new-agey spiritual schlock. Or maybe he wouldn't. One thing is certain: nothing is permanent. If he were still alive today, there's no telling how the past decade would have changed him. Maybe he'd throw an arm across my shoulders, give me a smile, and say, "Hey, whatever gets you through."

letting go

One afternoon in October 2006, almost exactly a year after Tim attempted suicide, my phone rang. It was an Alabama area code, but I didn't recognize the number.

"Is this Kelley?" a male voice drawled.

"Yes. Who is this?"

"You probably don't remember me. I used to be friends with yer brother. My name is Zeke."

"Sure, I remember you." The truth was, I only remembered his name. Who could forget it? He was one of the boys Matt had dragged home when we'd first moved to Alabama, the person who'd introduced him to Tim. Zeke cleared his throat on the other end of the line, and it hit me. Oh God, Tim. He had been in a downward spiral for the past six months. Ashley had terminated the pregnancy and broken up with him. His emails had been peppered with tales of heavy drinking and drug use. I hadn't heard from him in a month, since I'd told him I thought he needed help. And I knew, right then, that Zeke wasn't calling to tell me he'd gotten it.

My heart must have been beating, but I couldn't feel it. I couldn't feel anything.

"What happened?" I whispered.

"Well, I got some bad news." His voice began to break. "It's Tim. He's dying. He took an overdose. He's in the hospital, and he's not gonna make it."

And then I felt everything. The massive contractions of my

diaphragm, the wet heat of tears on my cheeks, the pounding of blood in my veins, and the jagged stream of oxygen trying to reach my lungs.

"You were one of the names he said, when he said he was sorry."

"When?" was all I could get out.

"It was yesterday. His brother got him to the hospital, but it was too late. I'll call you if anything changes."

I nodded my head, and managed to spit out, "Okay."

"Kelley, I know I don't know you, and this is gonna sound kinda stupid, but I love you."

It *was* kind of stupid—I couldn't even remember what this guy looked like—but it made me cry harder, because I knew exactly what he meant. I didn't care if it was stupid.

"I love you, too."

I hung up the phone, pressed my forehead into the desk, and gave myself over to the crying. One thought echoed in my head, my brain unable to process anything else: *I can't believe this is happening again.*

I opened a window in the living room. A storm was coming. Thunder tumbled across the sky, and a sharp blast of cold air blew in and prickled the skin on my arms. Clouds the color of ashes swelled. It was surreal. Only in the movies did bad weather coincide with bad news. The day we put Matt in the ground there were no black umbrellas. The sun was shining, the birds singing. The grass was green and the flowers had pushed their way up through the dirt, lifting their unfolded petals toward the sky.

I had called my mother right after hanging up with Zeke, and she had, in turn, called Lorraine. Tim was in a hospital in Birmingham, Lorraine said. He was conscious, he knew he was dying, and he was angry. He said his brother, who'd found him on the floor of his bedroom nine hours after the overdose and had taken him to the emergency room, should have let him die. His liver was failing. The doctors didn't think he would make it past a week, ten days at most. But of course it could be sooner.

I thought about what I had to do—fly down to Alabama and say goodbye. People who lose someone suddenly always say they wish they could have said goodbye. I'd said it after Matt died. And now that I had the chance that so many people dreamed of, I realized I didn't want it. Memories of my brother's death rose in my throat like vomit. *Please God, please let Tim die before I get there.* The thought left behind a wake of shame. How could I wish death on anyone? How could I wish death on a friend? Still, I couldn't stop it. It flew around my mind in slow circles, a banner behind a tiny airplane of human weakness. It was terrible, and it was true. I couldn't say goodbye. I couldn't stare death in the face, Tim's face. I couldn't lose another person to suicide.

I got on the computer and looked up flights to Birmingham. I knew I couldn't handle much. I didn't have it in me to sit by his bedside for a week and watch him slip away. So I found a flight that would get me in early Friday morning and get me home Friday night. That meant two more days to get ready, to figure out how to say goodbye. *Or,* the tiny airplane's new banner read, *two days for him to let go before you have to.*

I called Zeke to tell him my plan and to get directions to the hospital from the airport. When I told him about my flight, he said, "Yer only coming for one day?"

My stomach folded over. What did he want from me? I wanted to stick up for myself, to tell him about everything I'd been through the last two and a half years. What it was like to relive the death of my only sibling while grieving the impending death of my friend. But Zeke had unleashed a tidal wave of guilt, and I allowed myself to be swept away.

"Well, I guess I could stay until Saturday . . . ," I said.

"Yeah, I think that would be better."

I booked my flight, leaving Chicago early Friday morning and returning Saturday afternoon. Zeke arranged for his brother to come and pick me up from the airport because he wouldn't be there. It turned out Zeke was in a wedding and would be busy all day Friday and Saturday. I spent Wednesday and Thursday crying, writing in my journal, and talking on the phone with my therapist. Saying goodbye would be hard, would be horrible, but I decided I was ready. And then my mother called me Thursday night. She and my father happened to be in Alabama that week visiting friends, and they'd driven to Birmingham to see Tim.

"How is he?" I asked.

"Well, he looks pretty good. A lot better than I thought he would, anyway. He's hooked up to a lot of machines, but he doesn't look that bad."

"What did he say? Is he still mad?"

"He said he wants to be dead, he can't wait for it to be over."

"Jesus. How's Lorraine and everyone else?"

"They're . . . coping."

"God . . ."

"Well, there's one more thing."

"What?"

"The doctor said not to get our hopes up, but there's a chance he . . . He actually got a little better."

"*What?*" I held my breath.

"The doctor said that sometimes this happens right before a patient dies, but it could mean . . . he might make it. They'll know more tomorrow."

"Does Tim know?" I felt my eyes widen and my mouth fall open. "No."

I exhaled and sat for a moment in silence, shaking my head. "Um, okay . . . I guess I'll call you tomorrow when I get there."

I hung up the phone and kept the TV muted. I'd spent the last three days preparing for his death. And now he was . . . I didn't know what to think. My tiny airplane started dropping bombs: *Who does he think he is, jerking us around like this? If he isn't going to die, why am I flying across the country? My friendship, my concern, my worry haven't helped him. What the fuck does he want from me? What more can I do?*

The shame I'd felt earlier morphed into disgust. First I had wished that Tim would die before I saw him, and now I was angry that he might live? I told myself that I was a cruel, sick excuse for a human being. Not surprisingly, that didn't make me feel any better. It also didn't come close to the truth. I was scared, grieving, and powerless, and Tim was making it impossible for me to pretend that I wasn't.

I didn't know that then. I only knew that I would have given anything for an excuse not to board that plane.

The next morning I arrived in Birmingham, trudged up the incline of Terminal C, and saw a guy in khaki shorts and a polo shirt standing alone at the edge of security. I figured he must be Zeke's brother because his was the somber face in the crowd of people talking and laughing, waving and pointing to people they knew and missed. His eyes searched the crowd for a red Adidas T-shirt and blue jeans, and he gave me a wave. Nervous smiles, introductions, an awkward hug. I finally spoke the question that I'd been asking silently all morning: "How is he today?"

And Zeke's brother said, "He's going to make it."

———

I stopped in the doorway of Tim's room. He was as thin as he had ever been. Atop his head was a layer of light brown fuzz that descended via sideburns and bristled along his jaw and chin. I had never seen him with facial hair; his skin had always been so smooth, I'd assumed he didn't have any. His forehead was dry and flaking, and there was a crust of blood around his right nostril. Lorraine had said they'd removed the tube that morning.

"Hi," I said.

"Hey."

"So, you're going to be okay."

"Yeah."

"Do you feel better about that today? My mom said yesterday that you were pissed. That you wished no one had found you."

"Yeah, I feel better." He kept his head straight, but his eyes shot from ceiling to window, ceiling to window.

"You know this is a miracle, right? Maybe you're still here for a reason."

"Yeah, maybe."

"Tim, I think you're supposed to be here. Your family needs you here."

He shifted restlessly. I could tell that he didn't want to talk about it, but I didn't care. The anger from the day before was still there, smoldering like ruins.

"You need to make a change. I know you know that. You need to let people help you. Everybody gets help, Tim. I know it doesn't seem like it. I know it seems like 'normal' people don't need anything. I know because it seems like that to me sometimes, too. But they do need help, and they ask for help. Let us help you, okay?"

He didn't say anything. I put my hand on his shoulder and leaned in front of his face. He looked directly at me.

"I'm really glad you're okay," I said. He looked away.

"Yeah," he said. I stepped back and sighed.

"I know everyone else wants to see you, so I'll go get them."

Tim's parents were waiting in the hall. Zeke's brother was there, too, and so were Tim's brother and sister. They spilled into the room, settled around the bed. I could see the relief on their faces, skin that had been pulled tight for days finally relaxing, mouths that had been pressed into white lines finally smiling. In the middle of it all was Tim, his eyes cold and glazed, his face like hard wax.

A memory tightened my throat. I'd seen that face before. Arms across his chest, eyes like wet steel, my brother sitting silently in a chair behind a plastic table.

I was sure, in that moment, that Tim would attempt suicide again, over and over, probably until he succeeded. And I understood, for the first time, that you can't help someone who doesn't want your help, can't save someone who doesn't want to be saved. I understood my brother had not wanted me to save him. I understood that I had to let go.

I'd rekindled my friendship with Tim in the hope of glimpsing a bipolar life—and I'd gotten the full frontal. Tim had showed me his fears and desires in a raw, honest way that my brother never had. He'd shared with me the pain of stigma, the loss of hope, his bright-burning creativity, and his huge heart.

But I still knew next to nothing about Matt's illness. Because even though they shared a history, a diagnosis, and an unrepentant facial expression, Tim was not my brother. His life was not my brother's life. His illness was not my brother's illness.

And neither was mine.

This realization has bled so fully into the past that it seems like I've known it all along. As though I created a catalog of Matt's and my similarities subconsciously, to keep him safe before I ever knew he needed keeping. This re-remembrance, then, of our differences should have eased my fear of fate. I think it has. But it's taken more than Tim's attempt, more than the inventory of divergences between Matt's life and mine that surfaced afterward. It's taken the passing of years—each one a victory, each one a surprise. Sometimes time sticks, sometimes I can't imagine how I'll make it through another moment, and sometimes time flies so fast it's hard to catch my breath and there are so many reasons to be alive that I want to cry.

———

Tim sent me an email about three weeks after his attempt. He said he had learned his lesson and was no longer bitter that he'd been unsuccessful. He had a new lease on life, and when his depression returned he would be mature enough to deal with it. Then he said that he was back at the bars, though only drinking Diet Coke. And he had enough money for a car. And as soon as he bought one, he was going to get a job. And he was starting three new bands. And he had a new girlfriend. He closed the email with an apology and a promise never to attempt suicide again.

I wanted to be the kind of person who could hold Tim's hand while he fell apart, the kind of person who could be strong for him when he couldn't be strong for himself. Maybe if Matt hadn't killed himself I would have been able to. But he had, so I couldn't.

It wasn't easy, but at least I had the comfort of a country between us and the safety and sterility of a white screen to hide behind. I told Tim I was sorry. I told him I would always think of him, love him, but that I might never be able to trust him again. I told him that I understood why he'd done it, but that it was just too hard for me. I told him that Matt's death had destroyed me, and that our friendship was keeping me from healing. I asked him to give me space. I asked him not to call, not to write. And I asked him to forgive me.

two years, six months, and twenty-five days

Though Ryan and I had met in Alabama, he was actually from Michigan, too, and the bulk of his extended family still lived in the Detroit area, just like mine. This meant that holidays were divvied up between four families—a whirlwind of scheduling, eating, and chatting that left both of us stressed and exhausted, even in the years before Matt died. In the fall of 2006, I asked Ryan not to tell his relatives that we were going to drive to Michigan for Thanksgiving. We were going back again for Christmas, and I promised him we could see everyone on his side then.

I should have told him why. I should have told him that I needed space, that I was planning to go to Matt's grave alone for the first time, and that I was afraid. But I didn't want him to know. I didn't want anyone to know. Somehow I was convinced that if my visit to the cemetery wasn't a secret, it wouldn't work. That if my parents and husband knew my intentions, I would feel them standing next to me at Matt's grave. I would feel their grief, and once again it would keep me from releasing mine. So I didn't say a word.

The phone rang one night a couple of weeks before Thanksgiving. I muted the TV so Ryan could answer it.

"Hello? Oh, hi, Grandma!" He gave me a wave as he carried the receiver into the other room. I turned the volume back on, hearing his voice every now and then in the silence between commercials. A few minutes later, he came back into the room.

"Okay, we'll be in town for Thanksgiving, so we'll probably see you then. Bye!"

I muted the TV again and glared at him. "What the hell was that?"

"Oh, it was my grandparents," he said, looking over his shoulder at the TV.

"Yeah, but why did you do that?"

"Do what?" He looked back at me, and I raised my eyebrows.

"Tell them we would see them over Thanksgiving?"

He shrugged. "I just thought maybe I would go and see them, maybe for breakfast or lunch on Saturday."

"But you didn't say *I'll* see you, you said *we'll* see you."

"I did? Well, you don't have to go."

"But you said *we*, and now they'll be expecting me."

"So? I don't get what the big deal is, anyway. It's not like we have anything else going on," he muttered.

I should have told him. I should have told him then. But I didn't.

"The big deal is that we talked about this. I asked you specifically not to say anything. I told you I wanted to have a quiet, easy holiday for once."

"You're right," he said. "I'm sorry, it just kind of slipped out."

He was still standing in front of me, only looking directly at me now. I could see that he meant what he was saying, that he felt bad. I knew he probably even meant what he'd said about my not having to join him, though typically equality in family visitation was a touchy subject with us. Still, I would go. I wasn't ready to explain the real reason I didn't want to.

He sat down in the chair beside the couch and unmuted the television. *Just a few more weeks*, I told myself, *and it won't matter anymore. Just a few more weeks, and it will all be over. It will be better.*

━━━━━━━━━

My memory of Thanksgiving Day that year is like a video without sound. I don't remember what I thought or felt. I recall rolls and potatoes, a green-bean casserole and turkey. Pie. A football game on the TV in the living room.

I don't know what happened the next morning. Why, instead of going to the cemetery then, I decided to go on Saturday, knowing that I would be pressed for time. Knowing that I had agreed to spend the afternoon with my husband's grandparents. Knowing that I would then have to go to dinner at my cousin's house. Knowing that I wouldn't have a moment's peace, a moment's solitude, until late that night. Maybe I was so certain that the visit would make me feel better, I thought none of that would matter.

What I do remember is this: by Friday afternoon I'd figured out that there was no way to keep my visit a secret. My plan was to drop Ryan off at his grandparents' house, go to the cemetery, and then return to the grandparents' house for lunch. I wouldn't have to tell my parents that I was going, but I would have to tell Ryan. I pulled him into the guest bedroom and shut the door behind me.

"Is it okay with you if I go to the cemetery tomorrow while you visit with your grandparents?" I mumbled.

"I guess. Are you still coming to lunch?"

"Yes, I'll come back and meet you for lunch. Where are we going?"

"The Olive Garden."

Jesus. The Olive Garden? Am I really going to visit my brother's grave by myself for the first time and then have lunch at the Olive Garden?

I rolled my eyes. "Okay, fine. Can you help me get directions to the cemetery?"

"Of course."

I slipped from the guest bedroom to the computer room and dragged him along with me. We sat at the computer together and pulled up a map.

"It looks like the easiest way to get there from my grandparents' house will be to take Telegraph—"

"No, I don't want to take Telegraph."

"Why not?"

"*Because*—I just can't. I don't *know* it. I don't want to get lost."

"Um . . . okay. Well, look, I don't really know what else to do, so why don't we just ask your parents?"

"*Why can't you just help me?*" I hissed.

"*Because I don't know these roads either,*" he hissed back. "I'm going to ask your parents."

He pushed up from the chair and left the room before I could think of a reason to stop him, and the next thing I knew, my dad was looking at the computer screen over my shoulder. I crossed my arms tight over my chest and clenched my jaw.

Fuck. Now I would feel my father at the cemetery, rocking back on his heels, exhaling through his nose, and passing me an invisible box of Cheez-Its.

"So you want to go from Dearborn?"

"Yeah."

"Well, the easiest way would be to take Telegraph—"

"*No,* I do *not* want to take Telegraph. I don't know that road. I just want to go the simplest way."

"Uhhh, I guess you could take Cherry Hill to Beech Daly and Beech all the way to Ten Mile. It's right there at that intersection—"

"I know. I remember."

"Okay, but that's going to take a lot longer. Telegraph would be faster—"

"I'll take Beech. It's *fine.*" I closed the browser.

"Oh—uh, didn't you want to print out some directions? Do you want me to draw you a map or something?"

"No, I'll remember."

He left the room, and I closed the door behind him. I sat in front of the computer, stared at the screen, and tried to slow my breathing. If I had been home, I would have screamed. I would have broken something. I would have thrashed and kicked and melted into the cool tile floor of the bathroom. I don't know why I didn't there—my parents had seen me do it a hundred times before. But ten years had passed since the early days of my depression. Now I was, supposedly, an adult.

I took a deep breath, opened the door, and walked into the kitchen. My mother was waiting for me. She held what looked to be a xeroxed pamphlet.

"I thought you might want this." She handed it to me and I unfolded it. It was a cemetery map.

She knows, too?

She came around to my shoulder and pointed over my wrist. "You want to bear right when you get past the gates, over that bridge—"

I jerked the map down. "I know. I remember."

Her tears. They would be coming with me now, too.

Fuck. Fuck fuck fuck.

"Thanks," I said, nodding and folding the map. "I'll go put this in my purse."

I went back into the guest bedroom and closed the door. I put the map in my purse and sat on the floor with my back against the bed, my legs drawn into my chest, my forehead pressed against my knees. I thought if I pulled, squeezed hard enough, maybe I could fold in on myself. Maybe I could disappear.

―――――

I couldn't sleep that night, and I couldn't stand lying next to Ryan's heavy body, the faint whistle of air in, out, in, out. I went to the extra bed in the computer room. It was my parents' old bed, the bed Matt and I had used as a trampoline on early childhood Saturday mornings to wake up Dad. I lay flat on my back and put my forearm across my eyes. My chest was on fire, something like the sting left by copious vomiting. *Heartburn*, I told myself.

What the hell is wrong with you? Just keep it together. This is not a big deal.

I waited for the sweet release of mind over matter.

It didn't work.

I crafted a generic plea to my subconscious, God, whoever was listening.

Please, please, I really need to sleep.

I waited for the sweet release of mercy.

Nothing.

I rolled onto my side, curled into the fetal position, and waited for dawn to break.

―――――

The next morning, every clank of spoon against bowl stabbed my eardrums. Every scrape of chair, rustle of newspaper, click of my father's jaw while he chewed, reverberated on my skin. I wanted to scream, "SHUT THE FUCK UP!" and then realized that I hadn't noticed my father's jaw since I was a teenager, after we'd moved to Alabama.

"God, can't you do something about that?" I'd said one night over dinner, my lip raised in disgust.

"About what?"

"That hideous noise your jaw makes."

"What do you want me to do, exactly?" he'd said, his eyebrows raised and nostrils flared.

"Get surgery or something."

"You want me to get *surgery* because the sound of my chewing bothers you?"

"Yes."

"No."

"Well, I can't listen to this," I'd said, getting up from the table. "It's making me sick."

That morning all I said was, "I think we need to get going."

My father looked up from the paper. "What time do you think you'll be back?"

"I don't know."

"Because we're leaving for your cousin's house at four."

"*I know*—we'll be back in time."

"Okay, I guess we'll see you later."

Ryan drove. After he pulled into his grandparents' driveway and got out of the car, he waited for me by the driver's-side door. I pushed past him, fell into the seat, and slammed the door. He motioned for me to roll down the window. I did, and he said, "Okay, so you just back out and go that way and make a right at the light—"

"*I know.*"

"Okay, okay. Call me if you need anything. I'll see you around noon. I love you."

"*All right*, fine. See you later."

I pulled away without looking in my rearview mirror. I didn't want to see him standing in the driveway, looking after me.

In the back of my mind, I still hoped that I could leave my husband in the driveway. My father at the breakfast table. My mother in the kitchen. Maybe there was a chance it would work, that I'd open my mouth, my heart, and release all that anger and pain into the wind like the wail of a bagpipe or a bunch of balloons.

I made the requisite turns, and in a matter of minutes I was parallel with my past, only two miles west of the town where I'd grown up, where we'd grown up. The real reason I didn't want to take Telegraph.

Each intersecting street was a rung on the ladder of memory. Warren Road: my uncle's freezing-cold basement on Christmas morning in the years after the move, my brother and I wishing each other merry Christmas across the dark from the couches we slept on when we came to visit for the holidays; Ann Arbor Trail: two children finally old enough to walk the five blocks from Grandma's house to the playground, holding hands each time we crossed the street because we'd promised Mom that we would; Joy Road: Franklin High School, where I'd had a nearly perfect freshman year before learning the meaning of change; and then Plymouth Road. One left turn, a few minutes, and a right on Haller, and I could be in front of our house—the half-brick, flat-faced, two-story colonial, third lot in from the dead end.

But I didn't turn. I drove straight past the past, over the steady rush of the interstate, through the stretches of brown earth stripped bare by recently spreading subdivisions, beyond the point where the cracked pavement was flanked by evergreens, under the swinging traffic light at Ten Mile Road where Beech dead-ends into the yawning black gate of Holy Sepulcher Cemetery.

I entered and stayed to the left. *Over the lake, to the right, past the mausoleum, follow the curve* . . . but there were splits in the drive I didn't remember, and I got lost. I pulled to the side of the road and dug the map out of my purse. I was at the back of the cemetery and too far center, but if I kept heading east I would find it. I drove slowly, the upside-down map pinned to the top of the steering wheel by my thumbs, and my eyes flashed from road to map, road to map, until I saw the tree. That I remembered—short and squat, with rough, splintered bark.

I pulled up next to it, and as soon as I cut the engine off it occurred to me: *I should have brought flowers.* I thought for a moment about going to the flower shop across the street from the entrance, but I looked at the clock, remembered the Olive Garden, and decided that I didn't have time.

When I got out of the car, I noticed that the grass, which had looked pristine and emerald through the foggy car windows, was actually soaking wet and littered with goose shit. I walked to Matt's marker and stood next to it for a moment, staring at the ground. Of course. Of course I had assumed that I would just sit there on the grass. Of course I had driven for an hour without noticing the slick pavement and darkened bark of the bare trees. I had a memory of driving around for a few months with a lawn chair in the trunk of the car and thought that if I focused hard enough I might be able to will it to reappear. I walked back. All I could find was a plastic grocery bag.

I couldn't bring myself to sit on his grave, so I spread out the bag to the right of the headstone and sat cross-legged. This was it. The moment I'd been waiting for all those months. No one was there. No other mourners. No husband, no father, no mother. I didn't feel them, like I'd feared I would. I was alone.

I waited for the pain to rise, for the tears to come and wash me clean, for all the guilt, the fear, the loneliness, the helplessness, the rage, to burst out of me and float to the sky, twirling ribbon tails all the way to heaven.

But nothing happened.

I looked at the stone, thought about tracing his name with the tip of my finger.

Say something.

But my throat was tight, frozen. I sat until my ass was wet and cold. I looked at my watch. Fifteen minutes had passed. No beer, no Cheez-Its, no husband, no parents, and I didn't feel any better at all.

So I left.

━━━━━━━

I picked up Ryan and followed his grandparents to the restaurant. An aunt and uncle joined us for lunch, which bumped our party up to six. The hostess escorted us to a large, circular table, and I settled between Ryan and his aunt. Within a matter of moments, Ryan and his uncle were engrossed in one of those impenetrable "business" discussions, so his aunt turned to me and started telling me about her recent move into a subsidized apartment building for senior citizens.

"I really love it. It's only the one bedroom, but I've got my TV and little fridge for all my ice cream. I took home a bunch of that leftover turkey, I'll be eating that for weeks!"

I forced a laugh.

"There's always something going on—movie nights, card games, field trips. They've got a bus that takes us to the mall once a week. And it's real close to the theater."

"Sounds nice."

"Oh it is, and . . ."

Her voice couldn't compete with the screaming in my head. *DOESN'T SHE KNOW WHERE I'VE BEEN? WHAT THE FUCK AM I DOING HERE?*

The waitress appeared at my elbow.

"What can I get ya?"

I looked at the menu. "Don't you have a soup-and-salad combo?"

"It ain't on the weekend menu. I can get it for you, but it costs more."

"That's fine."

"Are you sure? It's not really a good deal."

"I'm sure."

As soon as I snapped my menu shut, Ryan's aunt was talking to me again. Her timeshare, her kids, her grandkids. I smiled until my face hurt. Nodded over and over again. Our food came, and then there was talk of that. How good the steak was, take those leftover breadsticks home. I said "yes," and "mm-hmm," and "oh yeah?" Snuck glances at my cell phone under the table to monitor the time.

Finally we gathered our Styrofoam containers, pushed our chairs back from the table, and headed for the parking lot. Before we could get to our car, my husband's grandmother said, "You're coming back to the house for a while, right?"

"*We can't!*" I blurted, poking Ryan in the back.

"No, I'm sorry, Grandma—we have to go. We're heading to Kelley's cousin's house in a few hours, and we need to get back to meet up with her parents."

"Oh, okay."

"We'll see you in a few weeks, at Christmas."

We got into the car and started back to my parents' house. It was rising—guilt, fear, loneliness, helplessness, and rage pushing up into my chest, clogging my throat, swelling against the backs of my eyes. I fought it as hard as I could, but it was coming too fast, too hard, and as we turned onto my parents' street, I exploded.

"Pull the car over. PULL THE CAR OVER."

He did, and I started to scream.

"WHY DID YOU DO THAT TO ME? I told you it was too much, I told you I couldn't see everyone, and you made me do it anyway."

He sighed and wiped his hands down his face. "I'm sorry, I thought I told you you didn't have to come—"

"BUT YOU MADE ME FEEL GUILTY. You told me they wanted to see me. WHAT THE FUCK IS WRONG WITH YOU? WHY DID YOU DO THAT TO ME?" I pounded the door of the car with the flat of my fist on every other word.

"I'm sorry, they *did* want to see you. I wasn't trying to make you feel guilty."

"I HATE YOU. WHY THE FUCK DID YOU DO THAT TO ME? WHY, WHY, WHY?" I was screaming so loud that my throat tasted like rust. The edge of my palm started to throb, so I stopped hitting the door and buried my face in my hands. I kept screaming, but there weren't words anymore, only sounds. It went on until my face was hot and swollen, my voice gone.

In the first space of silence, Ryan said, "I think we're in trouble."

He was right. I knew he was right. And I knew it was my fault. We were in trouble because I was in trouble. My grief was destroying me, destroying us, and if I didn't stop it, if I couldn't stop it, he would leave.

I want to say that knowing this was enough to fix it. That I knew right then that everything I'd screamed at my husband was meant for my brother, the pain I hadn't been able to release into the sky that afternoon. I did know, eventually, and eventually I was able to explain that to Ryan. But it took a few more years of wading through grief, and some marriage counseling, before we truly understood how much Matt's death had shut us down—both as a couple and as

individuals. When we injure one of our joints, the surrounding muscles tighten in an effort to stabilize the injury and prevent further
harm. My heart had been broken, and our lives had tightened around
it. Rehabilitation was slow, difficult, and painful, but possible.

But in that moment, in the car, all I really knew was that the trip
to the cemetery hadn't worked the way I'd thought it would. Maybe
I'd always known it wouldn't; maybe that was part of why I'd been
so afraid to go.

Facing Matt's death wasn't enough—I needed to face his life. My
life. The life we shared and lives we didn't.

three years

My mother, fearful that the host site for my brother's blog would eventually delete or lock his account, printed out all of his entries. Years of words. I knew from the moment she told me she'd done it that I would eventually ask for those pages. I believed they were the key to understanding who my brother was and why he'd died. And I believed that understanding who he was and why he'd died would end my grief, thus returning me to my regularly scheduled life.

By the time of my solo cemetery visit, my grief was holding me prisoner. That was the fall I had begun tapering off my antidepressant, and in the weeks between Thanksgiving and Christmas I succumbed to full-blown withdrawal. I quit my job at the gym. At home all day, alone, I was supposed to be relaxing, resting, focusing on my mental health. Instead, stripped of all distraction, I was forced to acknowledge the grief I'd been trying to avoid over the last three years while in a state of chemically induced (or reduced, as it were) anxiety.

I didn't know about Buddhism or meditation then. I didn't know you could honor feelings, sit with them, breathe with them, accept them without judgment. But even if I had, even if I had been a reincarnated lama who had been raised in a monastery, I still would have needed something else. I couldn't face that void empty-handed. I armed myself with a pen. I began to write about my brother.

But there was only so much I knew, only so much I remembered. And grief had distorted my memories, revising them to support what

I most needed in the moment, whether it was blame, comfort, or connection. The more I wrote, the more I realized how much of Matt I was missing.

It was time: I asked my mother for his words—the printout of his blog, his creative writing folder, and the black Five Star Mead I'd stuck the label from his mailbox on, the one he'd written his suicide note in. When she and my father came to visit later that winter, she handed them over to me in a paper bag with raffia handles. It was so heavy that the scratchy ropes dug into my palm.

"Be prepared," she said. "It's his voice. You will hear him."

Her tone and the look on her face—pleading, serious—obliterated my resolve. I stuffed the bag into the cupboard of my desk and let it sit. Every few days over the next two months I'd open the door and stare at it, wondering if I should pull it out, if that day would be the day. And then I'd shudder with a rush of fear and close the door. There would be a right time, I tried to convince myself. There would be a day when the thought of his voice wouldn't cause my heart to hammer in my throat. I remembered the support-group facilitator and told myself it would be soon: the third anniversary was coming. Yes, I would do it then. I stopped opening the cupboard door and waited for winter to melt into spring.

<hr />

After my solo visit to Matt's grave, I'd managed to find the courage to tell my parents that I no longer wanted to go to the cemetery. It did nothing, I told them, but make me feel worse. They said of course, no problem, they understood.

So on April 30, 2007, the third anniversary, I was at home in Chicago, alone. I felt like I should write my brother a letter, listen to some of his music, watch the still–cellophane wrapped *Danger Mouse* videos he'd given me for my birthday the year before he died. He'd asked me if I'd watched them almost every time I'd talked to him those last few months, and disappointment had lowered the register of his voice when I'd told him I hadn't. I'd been so busy studying for my grad-school comps, then hunting for and starting the library job, that I hadn't had time. It had been easy back then to push things off until tomorrow, next week, next month, next year.

But thoughts about writing a letter, listening to his music, or watching the videos were nothing more than a distraction. What I really wanted to do—or at least what I thought I should do—was start to sift through his words. I went into my office. I opened the cupboard door.

I closed the cupboard door. April 30, 2007, was not the day.

I didn't write a letter, either. Or listen to his music, or watch the videos. But I did watch television: prime-time reruns all afternoon.

All I'd wanted those other years was to let the anniversary pass quietly, quickly, to stop replaying the ceremony of his death. But that third year—finally alone, at home, finally what I'd wanted—I couldn't escape the cycle. I found myself watching the clock, imagining his body hanging, the minutes and hours pushing toward its discovery as if it were happening right then, for the first time. As if the police would ring my parents' doorbell the following morning.

I sat in front of the TV for hours, waiting for five o'clock. For his friend to find him, in my mind. For the police to come and cut him down.

━━━━━━

I thought that after the anniversary things might turn around, that I'd find the strength to face Matt's writing. But his words sat in the cupboard of my desk all summer. I still looked in on them occasionally, expecting that one day when I opened the door I'd feel a pull, instead of my entire body contracting, recoiling. Summer began to ease into fall, and the leaves wilted in the heat, yellowed at their edges.

"Why don't you just try reading a few pages at a time?" my therapist suggested.

I shrugged.

"What are you afraid of?" he asked.

"Hurting more than I already do," I said. He nodded.

A month passed. Two. The air thinned, sharpened. The sun cut a closer arc, hurried to the horizon in the afternoons. I pulled my sweaters down from the top shelf of the closet.

"You're going to have to face it eventually," my therapist said.

"I know."

It happened, finally, in November. Almost exactly three years after I heard about three years.

I don't remember feeling ready or being pulled. I do remember the sinking flush of being overwhelmed. On my desk, a stack of paper nearly three inches thick: the printout of his blog. I decided I would three-hole-punch it and put it into a D-ring binder, to cut down on the risk of pages getting lost or out of order. I didn't have to read it, I told myself.

But as soon as I sat down, I was. I skimmed and I punched, skimmed, punched, skimmed, punched. There were entries about concerts and parties, world and local news and politics. There were comments from friends and pictures, links to other blogs. My mother was right. I heard him and it was hard. So hard it made me ache—head, neck, eyes, heart. My fingers grew dry from the rub of the paper, stiff from the constant bend of turning pages. But I couldn't stop. I skimmed and punched faster. I was searching for a post titled "Everything You Need to Know About My Suicide." I didn't find it.

But I found him, Matt. The boy, the man, the person beyond my little brother. The similarities between us and the many, many differences—in our illnesses, our personalities, our experiences and interpretations. Though I'd known there was much of Matt's life I'd missed, though I'd suspected constructing the narrative of our lost years, the years we'd spent apart, would change the way I saw him, I expected the bulk of the change to be confined to the end of his life. I was wrong.

As I read his blog that afternoon, as I read through his notebooks and stories in the months after, as I recovered memories long forgotten and collected never-before-heard stories from his friends, as I scoured medical records, looked at old pictures, and watched home movies, our entire history was rewritten. With each new piece of information I found myself going back, reliving the layers of our lives. Though they all moved toward the same end, it seemed there were countless beginnings and middles. I began to understand that the timeline I'd envisioned as split into two parallel tracks was now frayed into infinite strands. Or had always been infinite strands, waiting to be undone.

surfacing

a small, dark place

There was no easing in. As soon as I read the first page of Matt's blog, I fell headfirst into everything I'd been avoiding in the three and a half years since his death. And even though reading his words was every bit as painful as I'd feared it would be, I couldn't stop. I came back to them the next day, and the next day, and the day after that. And when I wasn't reading them, when I was too raw and too ragged and too torn apart by grief, I thought about them, the spaces between them, the motivations and moods behind them. I thought about the words he didn't use, and the feelings and fears that had kept them from the pages.

I had a routine. In the morning: breakfast. A run. A couple hours of mind-numbing TV. Lunch. A little more TV. And then the walk down the hallway to my office, where his papers waited on my desk.

If it was a good day, a strong day, I'd spend a few hours reading his words, combing my memory, taking notes, recording observations, trying to jam together a few more puzzle pieces. If it wasn't a good day, I'd write about how hard it was, how angry I was, how tired I was, how little made sense. I'd wonder what the fuck I was doing, why I was wasting my time, why I couldn't just move on with my life. If it was a bad day, I would cry. And if it was a really bad day, I would stay on the couch after lunch and watch reruns of *Law & Order* until the sun set and Ryan's key scraped in the lock and it was time to make dinner. Those days came far more often than I wanted them to, and I made them far worse than I needed to. I berated myself for being a failure. I let Ryan do the dishes, popped tranquilizers, and went to bed feeling hollow, weak, and ashamed.

This was the place from which I started healing. It was small and dark. Barely enough room to breathe.

And it was familiar. It was where I'd been stuck after we'd moved to Alabama, where I'd been when I'd seen my reflection stretch into infinity in Leah's mirror. I didn't know how much of it was depression, how much of it grief. There is a thin line between the two, as most anyone who has lost someone can tell you. But this time the space wasn't just mine. By immersing myself in Matt's life, I had plunged into his pain.

I've thought a lot about this in the years since then. How his absence allowed me to inhabit his experience without expectations. There was no pressure to help or fix—it was too late for that. All I could do was listen, watch. Day after day I examined the shards of suffering he shared, pieces of the shadow of the whole—something far larger than he could express. It was nearly unbearable.

It was also a gift. It was how I began to peel his illness, his past, his life apart from mine. To let him be more than my brother. More than my loss.

But first his words, his pain, were caves that I crawled into alone— meaning I didn't tell anyone what I was doing. Except, of course, my therapist.

For the record, he thought that keeping my forays into Matt's writing a secret was a mistake. It was the start of an emotional marathon, one I was running barefoot over broken glass, and those closest to me had a right to know why I was bleeding. Because even if I could keep the facts quiet, I couldn't stop myself from having, and expressing, feelings.

I'm inclined to agree with my therapist now. I'll add that telling people where you are and what you're going through usually results in cheerleaders on the sidelines, and even a few people who will run alongside you as far and as often as they can.

But at that time in my life, isolation was instinct. It had been for over a decade—since I'd first experienced depression. It was the easiest way to protect myself, and others, from my darkest, most difficult feelings. The reason was twofold: 1) I didn't want people to think that I was weak, sick, broken, or different, and 2) I didn't want the people I loved most to worry about me. Because that's what they did. After my first major depression and suicide attempt, I felt like people were watching me, waiting for me to fall apart again. There was fear behind the concern in my parents' eyes, and I hated it. So I closed up, pushed everyone away. Or at least I tried to. I was never as good at it as I wanted to be. Never as good as my brother.

It was especially clear in his creative writing. First-person narrators trapped in their heads, tortured by their thoughts, rarely interacting with others. There was one piece in particular, a dense deconstruction of the self, made up of shifting points of view, song lyrics, and quotes from the Marxist philosopher Georg Lukács. It was called "Alienation and Self-Loathing: The Story of My Pathetic Fucking Existence." It began like a fictional narrative, a father and son plowing in Germany. They had the same names as our great-grandfather and grandfather:

> "Scheisse . . ." Karl slammed his backhoe into the firm, unrelenting earth. He called his son Peter and told him to begin softening the ground. Peter stoically complied. The family was something of an anachronism in northern Germany. Most of the region was heavily industrialized and no longer was there much of a place in society for farmers. When Peter went with his father into the city, he could feel the irony of their existence as if they were shades of grey amid a rainbow field. The city was so active, so full of spontaneity, and each time they came back to it, Peter felt it had grown even larger, like the vegetables on their farm.

And then white space, followed by a quote from Marx's *The Communist Manifesto*:

> *A specter is haunting Europe—the specter of Communism.*

It seemed to be the story of a family on the brink of being consumed by industrialization. The death of a father and the birth of a son. But then the point of view worked its way inward, moved from third to second to first, and the city, seen from the inside, was deglamorized:

> *The city was disgusting. Garbage strewn about, toxins in the air—you couldn't walk around it without afterwards feeling the filth on your skin. And the hustle, the corresponding bustle, it was enough to drive a guy mad sometimes. You could see small strips of land on which various overstressed citizens attempted to cultivate a few tomatoes as well as some sanity. Every now and then I'd ride my bicycle to the woods and just sit and listen.*

More white space before the next section. The first person continued, but the words belonged to someone else. It was a stanza of lyrics from the song "Flamethrower Love," by the Dead Boys, a punk-rock band from the late 1970s:

> *I got a nuclear explosion*
> *Breathing down my back*

White space again, and then Matt's narrative returned. In the woods now, only he'd pulled back to the second-person point of view, jerked away from the first person as if he'd touched something hot or sharp:

> *The early afternoon sun would melt you away some days, just as it seemed to eradicate all life around you. The country is slow, it looks dormant. But "dormancy" implies the absence of some possible or past activity and really, you'd never be able to surmise what that might have been or would be. The country is just dead. You can walk half the distance you would in the city and it would take twice as long. A gelatinous, invisible medium precipitates from the earth and you have to push and push to get through it.*

The escape from the city was no escape, then; the nuclear explosion followed him wherever he went. Themes were emerging: 1) belonging—Peter's conflict between farm and city, Matt's conflict between city and country; 2) the struggle of life and its possibility (or failure) as redemption—Karl and Peter's unrelenting soil and the ever-growing vegetables on their farm, the tomatoes grown in the city to cultivate sanity, the scorched atmosphere of the woods; and 3) the all-encompassing (though not directly expressed) need for relief, the search for peace.

Another break and then the quote from Lukács. Though fewer than two hundred words, it was a monster of a thing, the most solid and stubborn fragment yet. A brick wall of theory that took me months to dismantle. The fallback to thoughts over feelings, intellectualism as armor, I thought at first. All those arguments Matt liked to have about politics, those heated discussions that fooled me into thinking he was opening his heart. But I think now that he was using theory as form, something to explain all that white space, all those broken pieces.

The quote was about reification (regarding something abstract as a material thing), the fetishization of commodities, and the isolation, despiritualization, and atomization of the individual. Atomization: to reduce to atoms. To break into fragments. To subject to bombardment with atomic weapons. Annihilation. A nuclear explosion breathing down his back.

Capitalism, my brother often said, was the root of all his problems. His atomized, alienated self and self-loathing.

Finding no peace in the city or the country, understanding his place (or lack thereof) in society, he embraced first person in the next section—withdrew completely, maybe hoping to salvage himself. Or at least to escape the overwhelming external world:

There is too much around me sometimes. I want it all but end up taking nothing. Instead, I deprive my senses, retreat to my nucleus, repel my own progress. I'd like to garden, I think, but it's difficult to do while inside; plants need sunlight to grow and I hate opening my blinds.

Here he uses plants again as a metaphor for survival—impossible to thrive closed off from the world. He'd spent the last month of his life isolating himself, pushing friends away, drinking alone in his apartment nearly every night. His existence had become insignificant, he'd written in a blog entry, any interaction with the outside world pointless nonsense.

More white space and then the lyrics to another '70s punk song, "It's Not Enough," by Johnny Thunders and the Heartbreakers:

> I can count on diamonds, rubies as well
> Oh, big deal baby, I still feel like hell

The emptiness and insatiability of commodity fetishism. Finding no peace within or without, he gave in, gave up. More space, and then the final paragraph:

> Hatred is a hijacker. It is fuel and energy as well as direction and aim—the cause and the effect. Hatred is all that is needed and it is all that there is. No food or drink, hot or cold, left or right, only hatred. It's all I have, all I need, and all I want.

Hatred reified. When it's all you've got, you make it sacred. You make it everything. Shout it until the heavens you don't believe in shake. It's easier than continuing to hope for something you're sure you'll never have. And when every moment of your life is anguish, when the pills don't calm the storm, when even breathing fails you, to find peace is to die.

I would have told someone, I said to myself in the first weeks, months, years after his death. *I would have done whatever I had to do to keep living.*

But maybe I wouldn't have. I never had before. As a teenager I'd locked doors and sliced into my skin. As an adult I'd left emails and voicemails unanswered, canceled dinner dates and parties, to sit in the dim light of the television or cry on the floor of my bathroom. Not once had I picked up the phone, called a friend, and said, "I can't do this by myself." Not once had I sat in front of Ryan or my parents and said, "I'm afraid. I need help."

As I said, it took me months to make sense of this story, and by the time I did—probably because I did—I had told Ryan and my parents that I was going through Matt's writing. I had punched the first holes through the wall around my grief. And in doing so I'd made some cracks in the other wall, too. The one I hadn't even realized was there.

self-portraits

One afternoon during the fall of 2007, I sat sideways on the El and watched the trees grow smaller, morph into brick and mortar as the train sped toward downtown. It had been about a month since I'd started reading Matt's stories, poems, and blog entries, and I throbbed all over, as if I'd lost a layer of skin.

I needed a break from my brother's words.

I needed something beyond words, with their connotations and nuances, their lost contexts and hidden meanings. I needed a different kind of language.

I hoped to find it in a painting.

It had been six years since I'd taken Matt to the Art Institute—the only time he'd come to visit me. It had been the end of his freshman year of college and the beginning of my first summer in Chicago.

I'd met him at the airport. The hello was awkward, and the train ride back to my apartment was a stretch of unfamiliar silence broken occasionally by nervous spurts of small talk. I didn't quite understand. We hadn't even been living apart for a year. In Alabama over Christmas we'd picked up right where we'd left off—noogies and wrestling, headlocks and gut punches, scathing banter and inside jokes. I attributed the awkwardness to public transit. It was always weird, always quiet. People constructed private spaces with silence

and empty eyes to combat the sudden, overwhelming degree of close-
ness to strangers.

The city slid by outside the window behind Matt's head, and it was
odd to see him against a backdrop that was, for the first time in our
lives, only mine. Surreal. I noticed how different he looked, how much
like a man. His shoulders had broadened, and he had the thicker neck
and sharper jawline that boys get after they turn eighteen. Technically
I had witnessed the changes, had been there when his head had finally
risen above mine, when his voice had dropped, and when he'd started
shaving. But it was because I had been there that I hadn't seen it.
His face was such a fixture in my perception that its reality became
clouded by the shadow of the soft, round-faced, blond-haired boy he'd
been just before he tumbled over the puberty line.

There, on the train, his profile was hard angles and pores, wild
eyebrows and thick whiskers. The ghost of that boy was still there—I
could see it in his smile, his eyes—but the old blurry filter of memory wouldn't stick to this new face. Instead, the round-faced, blond-
haired boy became a placeholder, the face I saw when we spoke on the
phone, when I read one of his emails, when I told one of his anecdotes
to a friend.

The face I see still, in my dreams.

Maybe it was his new face that threw us off, that caused us to carry
our private spaces with us when we exited the train. Maybe I just
wasn't ready to see him as an adult. Maybe it was all in my head. But
whatever the reason, the cloak of awkwardness was real for me, and
it fanned a fire of panic. How were we going to make it through this
week together?

I had wanted to fill our time with as many activities as possible in
order to avoid those still, silent moments where the wall between past
and present was most palpable. But I didn't know what to do with this
new face, where to take it, what it might like. And when I asked him,
he shrugged and said, "Whatever you want to do is fine with me."

So I took him on an architectural boat cruise and shopping downtown. I took him to a record store in Lakeview and a movie in Old
Town. And then I took him to the Art Institute.

We saw the impressionists first: Seurat and Monet, Renoir, Degas.
My favorites. Explosions of color, filmy and beautiful. Art that didn't

demand too much from me, that told me I wasn't the only one who fuzzed the edges of reality.

Next we made our way to the contemporary section—the dripping shadows of Francis Bacon, the aggressive abstracts of Willem de Kooning. Matt slowed down there, studied each painting carefully. I tried to do the same, but I couldn't find meaning in the pieces, and the harsh lines and sharp colors made my eyes ache.

Matt stopped in front of Jean Dubuffet's painting *The Grand Arab*. A crooked section of blue sky cut across the top, and the remaining four-fifths of canvas were covered in a mixture of beige oil paint and sand. Etched in the center of the canvas was a human figure with a circle for the head and torso, a conical neck, and what looked to be the legs of a chicken. The figure was smiling and holding one hand over its heart. At the edge of the horizon, over the head, was the sun, a yellow circle with spikes coming out of it.

"This is one of the best things I have ever seen," he said, shaking his head with a grin. I assumed he meant that it was so bad it was good, and for a moment I felt like the wall was down, like we'd reverted back to our old selves, and I chuckled. But as soon as I did, I thought, *He doesn't mean it that way; he sees something I don't*, and the space between us thickened again.

Another room held some of Ivan Albright's self-portraits, numbers 1, 3, 4, 5, 6, 8, 10, 11, 13, 14, and 16. I followed Matt to that wall and glanced them over. They were hard to look at, number 13 especially. Background black as clotted blood, eyes buried in folds of sagging skin so wrinkled it looked pitted, scarred. It was the one Matt stood in front of the longest.

I retreated to a bench in the middle of the room and sat facing another of Albright's paintings, a massive canvas, eight by three feet. It was dark, mostly black. An ornate door with a green-and-pink wreath filled the frame. There was a hand on the left edge, just above the knob, holding on to the jamb. It was called *That Which I Should Have Done I Did Not Do*, and it felt like a funeral.

I turned back toward the self-portraits, where Matt still stood, one knee bent, arms crossed over his chest. I watched his shoulders rise and fall with his breath and wondered what it was he saw. I had that feeling, again, that I was missing something.

When he finally moved away from the wall toward the next room, I hopped up and followed, nodding in agreement when he looked over his shoulder, his face fixed with seriousness, and said, "Those are really amazing."

It was Albright's self-portraits I was after when I returned to the Art Institute in 2007. I got off the train at Adams and Wabash thinking about how Matt and I had split, how our private spaces had solidified over the two and a half years between that visit and his death. I wondered if I'd be able to see it now, that piece of heaven or hell or truth or life that Matt had seen in Albright's paintings. I wondered if I'd feel that pull, that connection he had experienced. My stomach twisting in anticipation, I climbed the steps between the patina-covered lions, walked through the trademark archways.

I searched the walls of the contemporary section—Bacon, de Kooning, and Dubuffet were still there, but Albright's self-portraits were gone.

His painting of the door remained. Dark, closed. The hand still curled around the frame, paused in regret for eternity.

Fortunately, I found a book of Albright's paintings at the public library. Four-by-five plates of the portraits were there, buried on the last pages. There were twenty of them, the book said, all created during the last two years of his life and donated to the Art Institute after his death. Self-portraits 1 through 17 were a raw, unfiltered celebration of decay, an embracing of impermanence. Albright had carefully cataloged, and sometimes exaggerated, every wrinkle, every broken blood vessel, every coarse gray hair. His eyes, ranging from round and wide to sunken in seamed, swollen skin, were glazed with rheumic film.

At first *Self-Portrait (No. 13)* was just as off-putting as I'd remembered. But the longer I looked at it, the more I saw. The background was blue, not black. There was softness in the eyes. His eyebrows were raised, as if we were in the middle of a conversation and he was surprised and interested by what I was saying. The harshness of the detail and sallow tinge of the palette were meant to make me feel a bit uncomfortable. After all, the portrait was raw mortality. I couldn't look at it without thinking about my own aging body, my own inevitable decay.

This, I think, was what Matt responded to. Albright wasn't afraid to show the truth, the weakness, of his flesh. Matt prized brutal honesty—he constantly sought to strip away the illusion of comfort. Often, he did this by making people uncomfortable. The hardcore metal and grind music he played (and listened to); the tough, pointed questions he asked. His heart broke when he witnessed suffering, but he didn't fear it. He didn't turn away from it, just like Albright didn't turn away from aging and death.

"I want a face that has been compassionate," Albright wrote of his self-portraits. "A face that has shed tears, . . . that has been alive with joy, . . . that opens the door to you. . . . A face that has faith—a wrinkled face, an old face, a face ready for death."

I believe that Matt saw Albright's intention. He did not, however, see Albright's last portraits, which were not on display.

Portraits 18–20 were created after the paralyzing stroke that would ultimately claim Albright's life. It was during the last three months of his life that he discovered a smooth face, one no longer defined by deterioration. A lightly sketched face with faded features. A face that knows death is not the demise of flesh but the relinquishment of it. A face with soft, mournful eyes, looking forward.

And what would my brother have thought if he had seen those drawings? Would the serenity in them, the surrender, have strengthened his resolve? Or would they have lit the tiniest spark of wonder? What is it like to weather the storm? To slip from the world slowly, one atom at a time?

<hr>

After studying Albright's portraits and returning to Matt's papers, I began to understand that, in some ways, the space between us had always existed, that while I was a child and a teenager I simply hadn't recognized it because I'd projected myself, my consciousness, onto everyone around me. I also began to realize that it was because Matt was different. I had been right in the art museum: he saw things in art, in music, in literature, in the world, that I didn't. That no one else did.

He felt very alone. And he was, in the way we all are. Every one of us sees the world uniquely. There are stories and feelings and truths in the lines of our faces that only we can see.

When my parents flew to New Jersey to claim Matt's body, they stopped by his apartment to take stock of everything we'd have to clean out. Mom told me a few days later that one of the first things she'd noticed in his apartment was a series of self-portraits, taped to the glass panels of the doors that slid between his bedroom and the dining room. The doorway where he'd pounded in the nails to hold his weight. The doorway where he'd died.

They were modified photographs, she said, something he'd done on his computer. "Horrible. His face was all distorted, and . . . I tore them down. I threw them away. I just couldn't look at them."

I told her I didn't blame her, and I didn't ask her any questions. But I wondered what they looked like and when he'd put them up. They hadn't been there over the summer, the only time I'd gone to visit him in Jersey. I wondered why he made them. If his own twisted face was the last thing he saw.

In December 2007, after finding the book of Albright's paintings, I decided I wanted to try and find my brother's self-portraits on his old computer. I needed to see his final face.

At my parents' house over Christmas, I slept in the room where most of Matt's belongings are stored, including his computer. During the downtime afternoon hours of Christmas Eve, I closed the bedroom door and sat at Matt's old desk. I turned the computer on, right-clicked on START, and went to EXPLORE. The pictures folder on the hard drive was empty. So was the document folder. I worried that my parents had wiped the drive, just like my mother had thrown out the pictures. I decided to do a general search with the term *self-portraits*. The magnifying-glass icon at the bottom of the page swirled while the names of files flashed and disappeared. Nothing, nothing, nothing . . .

Something—and *another* something . . .

But not photographs, paintings. Two paintings by Ivan Albright—some reassurance that the moment was important to him. To us. I smiled.

I noticed that Albright's portraits were on a separate drive, and when I accessed the drive I found hundreds of Matt's pictures. They were arranged alphabetically, the Albrights under *I* for Ivan. And a few rows down, in the *M*s, my brother's face.

His first face, the one I remember only from photographs tinged brown by decades. Chubby cheeked and smiling with two bright white teeth. I clicked on the image and a slideshow of Matt's face opened, infancy melting to toddlerhood, to the long blond–haired early teen years, to the thick-necked, dark-haired young man who'd ridden the train with me. He'd created it in the spring of 2003, about a year before he died.

There was also a later face. A photograph showing only his head and shoulders. His nose scrunched and mouth turned down, right eyebrow furrowed and left raised, left eye popping out under the raised brow. It was a face he'd made all the time, one that had always made me laugh. I clicked on the image, and an animated sequence began. Matt's mouth opened and spit out another copy of his face, which grew and covered the original face and then opened its mouth and spit out another copy. An infinity loop, just like the tunnel I'd discovered as a child in our bathroom mirror, and recalled in Leah's mirror the summer of my depression. He'd created it in the fall of 2003.

And then the portrait that my mother must have seen. The same face, only the nose was flattened, widened like it was being smashed against a pane of glass. The jaw and chin were inflated to twice their normal size, and the left eye bulged as if it were being pushed out from behind.

It was created at the end of February 2004, two months before his death.

I wondered if it was a reflection of the enormous pressure he felt, simultaneously swelling within and crushing without. I wondered if he'd left those portraits there for us to see, to help us understand. I wondered what they looked like to him and realized that I'd never before thought about the way my brother saw his face. If he saw it the way I did, layered with the faces of the past, like the animated evolution he'd created. If his darker, sharper adult face had felt as strange to him as it had to me. Or if the flattened, bulging face was the face he saw all the time, had seen all along. If it had haunted him in the mirror, like my reflection had haunted me the summer before my suicide attempt.

I imagined him in front of his computer, the room dark, his face glowing in the pale blue light of the screen. I could picture him stretching his features, knew there was music in the background and probably a can of beer next to the keyboard. But I couldn't imagine what he felt. What he thought. Was the portrait driven by a need? The nameless urgency, the silent knowledge that had guided my hand all those years ago? Or had he crafted it with Albright's deliberation, attempting to capture something specific, something that could only be found in pixels?

———

A few days after Christmas, I decided to look for my art portfolio to see if I still had my old self-portrait. I found it, and I was surprised. The shoulders were too big, out of proportion. And the bent head, the face I was so sure had been fierce, challenging, the embodiment of black infinity, looked tired. The eyes I remembered as upturned and glaring straight ahead in defiance and aggression were in reality looking slightly to the right. They were flat, yet somehow seemed as though they were about to spill tears.

It was a face heavy with sadness, a desperate face. Yet it was also a waiting face, a face with hope. It wasn't full of the dark absolutes I remembered. It wasn't even done with charcoal. It was soft pencil, smudged and washed-out shades of gray. Perhaps time had worn away the black. Or maybe it had never been as dark as I'd thought it was.

music and lyrics

By the spring of 2008, I was on a miniscule dose of Prozac as part of my step-down process and I was writing every day. I spent afternoons alternating between the pages of my Moleskine journals and a word-processing program on my laptop.

It was the first time I'd written regularly since I was a teenager. For nine months before my diagnosis of depression, I had scribbled furiously in spiral-bound notebooks. Writing was a release unlike anything else—except the few times I'd dared to dig the paper-thin blade of an X-Acto knife into my skin. I wrote stories, stream-of-consciousness narratives, the details of dreams. But mostly I covered pages with poems.

I'd studied poetry in school. I knew feet and meters, alliteration and assonance, triplet, quatrain, quintet. I knew verse and stanza, the structure of a sonnet. Haiku, epic, ode. Yet I never tried to bend my words, to build or smooth or sculpt. They came from someplace deep, they rumbled, and they exploded from heart to pen to page in a hot rush like lava. And though I hated the feelings that inspired them, I loved watching my poems come to life. Like so many millennia of people before me, I was making something tangible out of my experience. Making something out of pain.

But then, after my suicide attempt, after my medication was regulated, I discovered that the rumble was gone. Lava washed cool in a sea of serotonin. I didn't know there was poetry beyond fire, unfolding a single sound at a time like the petals of a flower. I didn't know that I could create by reaching outside myself, just as I could by reaching in. So I resigned myself to the words of others. I tore the pages from my notebooks and burned them in the bathtub.

I'm not sure whether I knew, at the time, why I cremated my work—it just felt like the thing to do. Deliciously dramatic and sorrowful. I was mourning, after all, keenly aware that my creativity had died. I was less aware of the bridge I was burning to myself. Less conscious of the belief that those words belonged to someone who was dangerous and damaged, someone who should no longer exist. I hadn't completed suicide, but I was determined to destroy that part of myself. I was going to be "normal."

Or I was at least going to try.

The first thing I wrote after Matt died was a short story about cleaning out his apartment. Though I hadn't written creatively in over a decade, it had erupted out of me in a single sitting. The rush was familiar, intoxicating, and frightening. What was I doing? Why was I doing it? And, more important, what would I do with it?

I had never asked myself those kinds of questions as a teenager. I'd filled my notebooks simply because I had to, and I'd hidden them under my mattress. They were a repository for all the parts of me I felt I needed to keep secret.

Secrecy was safety. Throughout my teens and twenties I rarely mentioned being on medication, and if I did I made it into a joke. I never spoke about my attempt, didn't tell anyone about the charcoal or the ambulance or the hospital. Ryan didn't know anything about it until I started letting him read my manuscript—two years after I started writing, seven years into our marriage.

It wasn't until the walls started coming down that I realized how ashamed I was of my past, how much I thought of my depression and anxiety as faults, character flaws that I was somehow responsible for. And when I examined that shame more closely, I saw it rooted in fear—fear that others would feel the same way about my illness that I did. When I began speaking about my struggles more openly, I found out that some of them did. But then I realized that it didn't matter. That, in fact, they may have been taking their cues from me. If I looked at myself with kindness and compassion, if I looked at my depression and anxiety as feelings, as facets of my humanity, maybe others would do the same. And if they didn't? Fuck them. Accepting myself came first and last. And it cropped up a whole hell of a lot in between.

I know now that sharing my story, baring my metaphorical notebooks for all to see, has transformed the way I see my illness and myself. It's also been a necessary element in resolving my grief. It's cut doors and windows into the walls I built around myself.

Would Matt have gotten here if he'd continued living? Would I have gotten here if he hadn't died? I add these to the list of Questions Without Answers. A plague of locusts in the early days, the Questions have morphed into the occasional butterfly, the brush of their wings a delicate breeze on an otherwise-still day, which passes almost as soon as it's felt.

My brother wrote stories, blogs, papers for school. But he was first and foremost a musician.

It wasn't until after he died, after I started writing about him and thinking about my own motivations for writing, the link between my creativity and my depression, that I began to look more deeply at his music.

He was eleven when he got his first guitar. It was as if one moment he was a kid with glasses, migraines, slicked-back hair, and a tight smile, and the next he was a kid with a glossy black Gibson strapped across his chest, bangs brushing into his eyes, and a full-face grin. It was like that guitar was a limb he hadn't known he was missing.

He practiced all the time, halting chords and reverb clambering down the stairs and refusing to be blocked out by the volume on the TV. One afternoon, just after the first mention of the move to Alabama tinged the air, when home was still home but everything would not always be as it was, I sat in the door frame of his bedroom and watched him.

"Will you show me how to play something?"

"Sure," he said, pulling the strap over his shoulders and getting to his feet. I sat on his bed and rested the base of the guitar on my thigh. He stood in front of me and positioned my fingers on the strings.

"Okay, put this one here, that one there . . ."

"What is this?"

"It's Pink Floyd, 'Wish You Were Here.'"

He showed me how to move my fingers, explained the frets and how to use the pick. I played it again, trying to follow his instructions, and again, and again, until I did it right.

"Cool," I smiled.

And that's all I thought it was: a way for him to be cool. I didn't know then that art was its own language. That pictures and sounds could communicate when words failed. And yet, somehow, even after I found refuge in my notebooks, even after I used paint and charcoal to give form to feelings, it didn't occur to me that Matt was doing the same thing through music.

It was partly because I was self-absorbed and a little clueless. It was also partly because music doesn't work quite the same way writing does. It takes a while to find your voice. Matt started out status quo: playing classic rock from the '70s and contemporary alternative. He shifted to punk and surf later into his teens. By the time he started regularly playing the music he wrote, he was entrenched in heavy-metal grindcore—loud and fast, the lyrics unintelligible.

I remember the first time I heard his band. It was winter 1999, and they had a gig at an independent-music store in Tuscaloosa. It wasn't a good place to see a show. The store was long and skinny, with narrow aisles between the racks of CDs and records. The register was at a counter just inside the front door, and the band had set up against the opposite wall. I didn't know what was usually in that space, because I didn't hang out there. I hardly ever bought music anymore, and when I did I got it from the Blockbuster Music in the strip mall with the TCBY. Matt, on the other hand, had graduated from indie- and used-music stores to obscure mail-order catalogs. We'd once bonded over Nirvana and Pearl Jam, Pink Floyd and the Doors, but he and I didn't talk about music anymore. We didn't talk about much of anything anymore. I had moved out that fall, into a studio apartment near campus with a southward-sloping linoleum floor, a stove without a pilot light, and a bathroom sink with separate taps for hot and cold water. Most nights I slept over at Ryan's house. I went home occasionally to ransack the pantry, wash clothes, or write a paper. I was completely absorbed in my new life, my "adult" life. A life he wasn't part of.

So I was completely unprepared for what happened when the boys started playing. It was loud. It was hard. It was fast. They screamed the lyrics into the microphones, Matt in a piercing falsetto that I would later hear termed, accurately, "dolphin-rape vocals." I couldn't make out a word. It reminded me of the moment after an airplane touches down, when the cabin fills with the roar of air fighting slowing steel and the rush spirals into your ears and rattles your chest, and you grip the armrest and grind your teeth because you're sure that the plane is about to burst into flames.

I think my mouth was hanging open.

I think that was the point.

I didn't know what to do. Was I supposed to dance? Bang my head? Tear out the throat of the person standing next to me and bathe in his blood while invoking the Dark Lord? The world was bright outside the windows. The tendons in Matt's neck strained when he screamed. I stood motionless and waited for it to end.

It occurs to me now that this music might have been the closest thing to what was going on in his head. Violent and incomprehensible, too fast and too loud to decode. This music might have been his version of the mattress, masking the truth of his illness. A place for him to show without showing.

It also occurs to me that we didn't listen hard enough.

But really, if one bares her soul on burned pages, if one screams his pain against an amplifier turned up to ten, there's only so much you can do.

———

I suppose music and poetry are two of the ways in which we are all just trying to wrap our minds and hearts around the experience of existence. We are reaching and falling and breaking ourselves wide open, and it's thrilling and terrifying, and there's so much we don't want to see. So much that we don't know how to say. In the end, sometimes we need someone else's brush to paint the final stroke, someone else's words to finish the sentence.

Matt's suicide note opened with a narrative, an account of his return to New Jersey from Tuscaloosa after Christmas. He described carrying his luggage home from the train station and the pain of trying to get it up the stairs. He created a scene of himself on his bed, back against the wall, writing, before he shifted into the note itself. In between, this small section:

> *I poured myself a glass of water & put on a record—something pretty & dark, but something that only seems pretty and dark to me. I don't know why, but it always works out that I'm the only person that can hear things in records like that. Like the Beach Boys. They depress the hell out of me, but no one else gets it . . . the undertones, the tortured voice of Brian Wilson . . . no one seems to remember the bleakness of "God Only Knows," "I Just Wasn't Made For These Times," & even the classic "Sloop John B."*

I didn't listen to those songs right away, the faint echo of their melodies in my memory convincing me that I knew them. It was a few months later when, reading a book, I came across a reference to "Sloop John B" and realized that I'd never really paid attention to the words. *Why don't they let me go home?* I heard after downloading the song. And then Brian Wilson's voice ringing out into nearly dead air, the music stopped save for a few tinkling bells:

> *This is the worst trip I've ever been on.*

peace

I sat down to meditate for the first time in my life two years after my brother's death—not because of the giant black hole of grief that had taken the place of my heart, but because I was having trouble sleeping. I might not have said that those two things were related. I definitely wouldn't have said that I was seeking peace. After my strict Catholic upbringing, I was, like my brother, antireligion: Buddhism wasn't even on my radar.

My practice began as an exercise in stress reduction stripped of spirituality. The particular process I used, called the Relaxation Response, was laid out in a book sent to me by my uncle. The front cover of the book purported a "technique that has helped millions to cope with fatigue, anxiety, and stress."

For the first couple of weeks I sat twice a day—first thing in the morning and then again around 5:00 p.m.—cross-legged on the guest bed, my back against the headboard, my neck resting on its curved edge. I closed my eyes. One at a time I implored my muscles to release—*relaxing the toes, relaxing the toes, relaxing the toes; relaxing the feet, relaxing the feet, relaxing the feet*—until I'd worked my way up to my head and face, all the while taking deep breaths in through my nose, out through my nose, in through my nose, out through my nose. After I finished relaxing my head, I began to repeat the word *one* in my mind—drawn out, sometimes, with my in- and exhalations; over and over again, sometimes, to match the rhythm of my heart. I slowed my repetition, and my heartbeat and breathing followed suit. Then a tingling started at the base of my skull, spread down my neck into my fingers and toes. I floated up into the darkness behind my eyelids, lingered in a kind of limbo for fifteen or twenty minutes, and then raised my head, prompting the flurried return of what I thought was my consciousness. It was surreal—akin to getting high. And though it was supposed to be strictly physical (a successful way to lower blood pressure, the book promised), it felt like more. In that floating darkness was the pull of the spirit, the separating of the conscious self from the body. Was it possible? After a childhood of turmoil and doubt in the Catholic Church; after an adolescence of anger, depression, and atheism; after an early adulthood of anxiety, fear, agnosticism, and heavy grief, was I capable of peace?

Giddy at the prospect, I told my mother about my meditation sessions. I was proud to be discussing the topic with her—the highest authority, as anyone who knows her will agree, on all things holy. Recipient of a degree in religious studies, adult faith enrichment educator, catechism teacher, Eucharistic minister, conversion sponsor, choir member, and Scripture reader, my mother is also a bit of a mystic. She frequently attends silent retreats at monasteries and participates in a contemplative prayer group. I asked her specifically about the tingling. Was it normal?

"Oh, yes, I've heard of that happening. Very impressive," she told me. "It usually takes people years to experience that kind of sensation."

Years? Right away I knew that something was wrong. I was in no way a spiritual prodigy. Impossible that I'd achieved anything ahead of schedule.

That afternoon I took my seat on the guest bed. I relaxed my body, slowed my breathing and my heart, and as I drifted I felt a dull throb and then the tingle at the base of my neck. I stopped thinking *one* and started thinking about the head rush I got after every session. Of course. As wonderful and peaceful as it felt, my meditative calm was nothing more than a lack of circulation—the weight of my head pressing my neck too far into the edge of the headboard. I moved to a chair and sat with my head perfectly straight, neck resting on nothing. I breathed, I repeated, and I stayed right where I was—anchored in the flesh, fully conscious—and feeling my lack of transcendence was a failure.

For most of my life, and, I have to imagine, for Matt's life as well, the concept of peace was tangled with the concept of God (which was, of course, bound by the concept of religion). This had everything to do with context. I have no doubt that the first time we heard the word *peace* was on a Sunday morning. Every Sunday morning. If not echoing down from the altar or lectern, then during a handshake with strangers: "Peace be with you."

Because we said it every week, because I learned to say it well before I knew what the word meant, I didn't really think about what I was saying. The "sign of peace" was just another function to be performed, another line in the script of Mass. Kneel, cross yourself, bow your head, pray. None of it meant anything to me. To either of us, as far as I know. While Mom knelt after communion with her eyes half-closed, a soft smile on her face, I dragged my fingernail across the back of the pew in front of me, dredging up a sparkly residue of varnish. I stuck my index fingers through the space between the backrest and the seat. The gloss of the wood created a reflection of each finger, the two halves disembodied, connected to their mirror images. If I angled my fingers they became Pac-Man mouths. I moved them toward each other, chomping. Right almost always ate Left.

I don't know what Matt did or thought to get through church. We figured out early on that as long as we were quiet we didn't have to pay attention, and it was much easier to be quiet lost in our own heads. Religion was just another thing he and I didn't talk about. Maybe because by the time church was over, by the time Tuesday-night catechism was over, by the time confessions and Ash Wednesday forehead smudges were over, we'd had enough. I know I'd had enough.

The Father, the Son, the Holy Spirit. Salvation, Mercy, Peace. Everything was synonymous with the flickering flame at the center of my heart I was supposed to feel but never did. No matter what anyone told me—my mother, the nuns, the priest—I knew it wasn't there. It couldn't be; otherwise, why did I feel the way I did every time we sat down for a service? Stiff, closed, shut down inside—which meant there was something wrong with me. It seemed I had no peace. And so, I reasoned, I did not have God.

It was a terrible feeling. Empty. Guilty. Scary. I hated to go to church, to be forced to face my failure, which made me feel even worse. If I hated church, did I hate God? Could I hate God? Should I hate God? I didn't tell anyone what I was thinking, especially not my mother. I could see the distress in her eyes every time I skipped Mass, every time I brought a book and sat in the stairwell of the choir loft while she sang. Even so, I tried to get out of going to church and catechism classes whenever possible, feigning illness, grumbling about boredom, or whining about the fact that Dad joined us only at Easter and Christmas (a tactic shot down by the explanation that he'd had to go every Sunday when he was my age, and that once I was an adult I could quit going, too).

I made my confirmation at age thirteen. For the occasion Mom baked and frosted a cake, iced it with the outline of a dove and my full name: first, middle, and confirmation. When we made our confirmations we were supposed to, through reflection and prayer, take on the name of a saint we could admire and imitate. I'd decided on Alexis—the female adaptation of Saint Alexander, I'd claimed, though all I really knew about Saint Alexander was that he'd had needles stuck under his fingernails. I just thought the name Alexis was cool.

There is a home movie of my confirmation party. I sit at the head of the dining room table, flanked by a couple of my friends. Aunts, uncles, and cousins have crowded into the kitchen, and Mom enters the frame, carrying my cake. It is covered in birthday candles.

"Happy confirmation to you . . . ," she sings to the tune of "Happy Birthday," and places the cake in front of me. She is grinning.

I blow out the candles and roll my eyes.

Three years later, after we'd moved to Alabama and right around the time my depression kicked in, Matt began his final year of catechism. By then I claimed to be an atheist. I worshipped anger, destruction, and misery. The emotions of LIFE, the stuff of reality. Happiness? Calm? The stuff of morons. People who'd been lobotomized by religion or people who were just too dumb to open their eyes and look around. The world was full of suffering. The foundation of the human condition was chaos. To buy into the notion of peace was to be a sucker.

Heaven, I used to say, would be boring as fuck. Floating around on clouds all day? Being absorbed into some kind of universal being? Who the hell would want that? I shuddered to think of it. Not that I wanted to go to hell, though my reasoning might lead one to believe that. No, I craved the chaos of Earth. Reincarnation was for me. If I'd believed in God, I would have prayed for it.

Having convinced myself that I was privy to a deep philosophical truth, I would never have admitted that all I was trying to do was validate my unhappiness. If despair was all I had, then I would make despair into a sacrament. It was the only thing that kept me from suicide. Until it didn't. Mental illness is at its core a state of unbalance, discord, the polar opposite of peace. And when every moment of your life is anguish, to find peace is to die.

Of course, I didn't die. I lived. And every day I swallowed little pink pills—Paxil, from *pax*, the Latin word for *peace*. The irony was not lost on me.

About six months after my suicide attempt, Matt finished his eighth and final year of religious education. Remembering my pouting, eye rolling, metaphorical and literal kicking and screaming, Mom and Dad let him choose whether or not he would be confirmed. He chose not to be. They discussed it, and that was when he told Mom for the first time that he didn't believe in God. Roughly a year shy of his bipolar diagnosis, he was fourteen years old.

———

In February 2004, about two months before his suicide, my brother wrote on his blog:

> *Bitterness is a huge waste of time. That's right, I said it! But goddamn, goddamn is it hard to abandon.*

Peace, peace is where it's at. I started reading Thich Nhat Hanh's 2003 book, Creating True Peace, and on a lot of issues the dude is right on. So I'm creating peace in my life, ending violence inside myself, enjoying breathing. It's all about the peace, maaaan . . .

Matt's copy of Thich Nhat Hanh's *Creating True Peace* was a gift from Mom—I knew because she'd sent me one, too. I called to ask her if she remembered having sent it to him, and if she'd done it for any particular reason. She said that during a conversation in February 2004, a week or two before he posted the blog about peace, he'd asked her how she managed to be so cheerful, so peaceful, in the face of such a messed-up world. Why, he wanted to know, did she believe what she believed?

She told him about an experience she'd had in her late twenties. It was a Sunday Mass, one the three of us were at together, no doubt. And when she went up to receive communion she was overcome, infused, by love. She felt, she knew, that love was going to be her future, and that the love she was feeling was her gift to give. And, along with that, she felt a powerful sense of belonging, interconnectedness with the universe.

"That experience," she told me, "kept me going through all those years. All those years until he died."

That experience, she told him—the experience of knowing she was loved, of knowing she belonged—brought her peace. She told him she hoped he knew that he was loved: by her, by many. That he was precious. She told him she hoped the love everyone had for him would bring him peace. She wanted desperately to impress upon him that peace was possible.

She got off the phone with him feeling good. Feeling like he was searching. Trusting that he could, would, find the balance that he sought. Then she sent him the book.

She asked him a few weeks later if he'd read it. He'd started it, he told her. She asked him if he'd practiced any of the exercises. He said he hadn't, and the conversation stalled. She let it go. They didn't talk about the book, or God, or peace, again.

I don't think she ever asked me if I'd read *Creating True Peace*. I hadn't. I might have skimmed the first few pages, just to get a feel for it, to have something to talk about in case she brought it up. But I knew it was not for me. While I had softened in the years since my attempt, content to acknowledge the existence of things I couldn't explain and to admit that the evolution of life was something greater than coincidence, I was still skeptical enough of faith to stop myself from asking questions that I knew didn't have answers.

I wasn't a spiritual person. I wasn't my mother. The chaos of my heart and head would not be ordered by mindful breathing, and that was okay, because even though I was nearing the seemingly postadolescent age of twenty-five, I didn't think I wanted it to. My bitterness, sarcasm, cynicism, and anger were tenets of my *self*, as beneficial as they were troublesome. They made me "edgy," they made me "real." I assumed they were the reason (everything except the anger, anyway) that most people liked me. It took Matt's death and my grief to admit that stability, happiness, and peace were not only "real" and acceptable, but also necessary. I wasn't my mother, would never be my mother, but that didn't mean I didn't need to change.

Still, it was years before the Relaxation Response morphed into an interest in deepening spirituality. Years still before that interest prompted me to pick up *Creating True Peace* and give it another try.

We all have Buddha nature within us, it says. Goodness and the capacity for mindfulness, calm, and seeing deeply into a situation. Smile at your anger, it says. Smile at your fear.

The prospect that people can change the tempestuous weather of their internal landscapes is so very tempting. And so very dangerous. I fear that to blur the line between conscious control and mental illness is to fall across it, inevitably to fail. On page thirty-five, Thich Nhat Hanh writes:

> *The next time you are troubled and upset and think you cannot survive, please use this simple breathing exercise to get back in touch with your own true nature, the nature of awakening*

and compassion. Please, do not give up. Mindfulness in action enables you to overcome all dangers.

I wonder if Matt read this. I wonder if he tried to smile at his pain, his insecurity, his sadness. If he tried to smile at his anger and his fear. I wonder if they smiled right back at him—grinned mouths full of pointed teeth that would tear him into pieces. That's what they did to me, at first. But the more I sat with my depression and anxiety, my anger, my jealousy, my fear, the more I saw how much I needed compassion for myself. When I could observe my pain without judgment, I saw it not as a ferocious beast but as a tired, lonely child who needed comfort and acceptance.

I don't know how far Matt made it into the book. I was hoping to find his copy, a dog-eared, notated, underlined window into his search. But I didn't. Since he mentions the breathing, I think he must have made it as far as page nineteen—where the first of many breathing exercises is laid out. A few pages later, in a section called "Meditation for Compassionate Listening," are the following mantras:

Breathing in I know we both suffer. Breathing out I want us both to have a new chance . . . Our suffering, A new chance

Breathing in I want to be happy. Breathing out I want you to be happy . . . My happiness, Your happiness

Breathing in I see us happy. Breathing out that is all I want . . . Our happiness, Is all I want

The first time I read these words, I pictured the two of us sitting cross-legged, facing each other and holding hands, breathing in and out. Something inside me shifted. Lifted.

I began to understand that peace wasn't what I'd thought it was. Peace didn't mean the absence of negative feelings—it meant cultivating the ability to acknowledge and honor them, to let them exist without trying to change them. Peace didn't mean I would never face another obstacle in life—it meant that I would approach the next obstacle with open eyes and heart, no matter how painful.

As I read what I have just written, I think, *Okay, this sounds way too easy.* It wasn't. It isn't. It took years, and almost every moment of it was awful. I frequently cried while sitting on my cushion, and there were many days when, overwhelmed, I quit. There are days like that still. The difference is that when those days happen now, I know they are not failures. I am not a failure. Like my thoughts, my depression and anxiety shift, change, pass like clouds. They are feelings, and feelings are not permanent. Nothing is permanent.

Sometimes I think of my brother when I sit. I still picture him across from me, with a smile easier than the one he wore in life, and I know that both of us have found some peace.

forgiveness

One summer afternoon, at the end of our first year in Alabama, Matt walked through the back door with a black eye. I was in the kitchen.

"What the hell happened to you?"

"Seth punched me."

Seth was one of the neighborhood kids. He was fifteen, a year younger than I was, but at least a head taller. Matt, at thirteen, was still shorter than I was, barely five feet.

"What? Why?"

"I don't know. We were playing basketball and I made a joke—I said something about his mom—and he just . . . hit me."

Matt touched the bruised swell at the crest of his cheek as he said this, and my heart leaped into my throat. An explosion of adrenaline surged through my body, my fingers shaking as I yanked open the junk drawer and dug out a D battery. Matt stared at me.

"What are you doing?"

"I'm going to kick his ass."

I marched out the back door and down the street, Matt at my heels. The pavement shimmered in the hot sun. Sweat ran down my forehead. I could see Seth standing in his driveway, holding his basketball. I can't remember if he was looking our way, don't know if he anticipated the consequences of his actions, if he felt sorry or justified or afraid. I only remember the smudge of his face in the distance, the pound of my heart against my ribs, and the satisfying heft of the battery in my swinging fist. I imagined what it would feel like smashing into his jaw. I'd never hit anyone before, not for real, not for revenge. I walked right up to Seth and stood inches away from his face (which I had to look up into).

My fingers tightened around the battery. I was breathing hard. My jaw was aching. All the muscles in my body tensed. I wanted him to move, to reach for me. I wanted him to lift his hand, because I knew if he did, I could show him that his extra inches didn't matter. His extra pounds would not save him. He could smirk at me if he wanted to, he could even laugh, but I would cause him pain. A knee to the groin, I thought, would drop him to the ground.

"If you can't hit someone your own size," I said, "at least hit someone your own age."

Seth took a step back. "Hey, man, I ain't gonna hit no girl."

"Really? Because you hit a little kid, and I'm not seeing how that's any different."

He looked over my shoulder at Matt, dropped the ball, and raised open hands. "I don't wanna fight, man. I'm sorry."

I thought about hitting him anyway, but the moment was gone. My tired, sweaty fingers were losing their grip on the battery. My muscles quivered and quit against the strain. Those inches and pounds would matter now. But I took another step forward anyway, got back into his face.

"If you ever, ever touch him again, I will fucking kill you."

I turned on my heel and walked back toward our house, Matt following at my side.

I wish I could remember what happened next. If Matt said anything to me on the way back, if I said anything to him. Sometimes I think the memory stops here on purpose so that for once I did my job—the job I'd heard about since Matt was nothing but a bump under Mom's shirt. The job I didn't sign up for. The job that doesn't come with a handbook. Take care of your little brother.

<hr />

For the first few years after Matt's death, I kept a running tally of all the ways in which I'd failed him. I think everyone who was close to him did. My tally included the usual older-sibling shortcomings—convincing him to give me presents on my half-birthday, winning every race and board game even if it meant I had to change the rules midplay, ignoring him, hitting him, calling him names, attempting to overshadow him in every possible way. My therapist said I probably wasn't nearly as bad as I thought I was. After a while I started to believe him—then I found Matt's psychiatrist's notes, wherein my brother described me as "a needy attention grabber." Touché.

If that weren't bad enough, my tally also included being the family pioneer into mental illness and suicide. I was convinced I'd started a pattern by setting a bad example. Even after it became clear to me that my brother walked his own path, marked by its own experiences and obstacles, I still assumed that my struggles with depression had siphoned the bulk of my parents' time and energy. This, combined with the fact that we'd grown so far apart—that I'd *let* us grow so far apart, I thought—made me hate myself.

The feeling was, unfortunately, familiar. I'd been overly self-conscious and self-critical for as long as I could remember. *Self-esteem* was one of the watchwords of the '80s, but every time my mother told me I was special, I knew she was wrong. I wasn't the smartest, the prettiest, the coolest, the most artistic, or the most athletic. I was awkward and overly sensitive—thin-skinned, as my dad said—and regulation childhood bullying rattled me to the core.

It only got worse as I grew older, especially after we moved to Alabama. The first few months in Tuscaloosa were a cascade of snubs, loneliness, confusion, and frustration. And even after I started making new friends, I was plagued by the pain of losing old ones. By anger at my parents and myself. Anger at all the people I met for not loving me instantly, for not making it easy, for not being the people I wanted them to be—the people I already knew.

I didn't know what to do with that anger. No one told me that I didn't *have* to do anything with it. And so I lashed out at family and friends, stabbing their softest spaces. In the heat of the moment it was a beautiful feeling, sublime—the only way I knew to drain the well of venom in my heart.

But after. After my voice went hoarse with the screaming, after I ran out of tears, the reality of what I'd said crept in and I sat alone in my room, drenched in shame. I didn't want to apologize, I wanted to reach into their memories and wipe them clean. I wanted to find a way to cut out the part of me that caused—and, worse, enjoyed—their pain. But I couldn't. So I said nothing.

I lived with that cycle of anger, guilt, and depression for nearly fifteen years.

It wasn't until after I started meditating, after I started reading Thich Nhat Hanh, that my anger began to change. Well, actually, my perception of my anger began to change. The more I sat, the harder I worked to become aware of my thoughts and feelings, the easier it was for me to see their root. I hated myself because I felt I wasn't good enough. I was angry because I didn't have control over my feelings. I worked on trusting that I was good enough, just as I was. I worked on believing that I had value no matter how I looked, what I thought or felt, what my occupation was. I was no better than anyone else—*but I wasn't worse, either.*

After I developed compassion for myself, it was much easier to be compassionate toward others. I was able to see that other people's anger, bitterness, and cruelty came from their pain—just as mine did. I was able to ask for forgiveness and to offer it. Most important, I learned to forgive myself.

───

A few weeks before his death, Matt posted the following on his blog:

> *Sometimes I think about all the horrible things I've done to people and I just want to fucking cry. Never will any of you know how much regret I have, how much sorrow, how indebted to you I feel! . . . I feel and always have felt torment at nearly every waking interval . . . I hate myself and I cannot apologize enough.*

The post triggered a memory I'd long forgotten. I've said many times that Matt and I didn't talk about our experiences with mental illness, but that isn't exactly true. There were times, maybe half a dozen in our house in Alabama, when we spent hours pouring out our hearts. The only problem is, I don't remember what we said. I remember where we were—almost always in his room, he on the bed and I on the floor or with my back against the doorjamb. I remember how it looked—late at night, wet darkness pressing against windows all the blacker against the white glare of the light. I remember how I felt—like we were sitting side by side in the clubhouses again; like, for a few hours, we really were made of all the same things; like his words were mine and mine his, the moment ours.

I've said we didn't talk about the move, but we might have. I've said we didn't talk about the meds, but we probably did. I tried for years after his death to recall what we said those nights, sure that there were answers there. That I had known enough to save him and forgotten. Sure, then, after trying and failing, that everything was lost. But after I read that post, the faintest trickle of a memory returned to me.

It began in my old bedroom, his room after I moved out. I was sitting in the doorway, the jamb pushing into my back and the familiar black pressing against windows that were no longer mine. I don't know why I was at home so late, why I hadn't retreated to my apartment on campus or Ryan's house. I don't know how I ended up in Matt's doorway, what season it was, or really even what year (he lived in my old room for two years after I moved out). I think it was his junior year in high school—around the time he began to change, around the time of his suicide attempt—because as we talked, he was crying.

I hadn't seen Matt cry since he was a little boy. He hadn't even cried when Seth punched him. He was telling me that he felt guilty.

"I think terrible things about people. I'm prejudiced, I'm judgmental."

"What? That's crazy. You're not prejudiced—you're friends with everyone."

"No, I mean it."

"Well, everybody does that. Everybody makes snap judgments about strangers. I do it all the time. My internal monologue is a total bitch. It's how you treat people that matters."

He shook his head. "I'm a terrible person."

"Just for thinking mean thoughts? You can't control the garbage rolling around in your head. Besides, I'm telling you, everyone does that. You gotta let it go."

So easy to give him advice I didn't follow.

When I think about that night now, when I think about his blog post, I am flooded with sadness and the protective older-sister urge that caused me so much pain after he died. I want to hold my little brother in my arms. I want to tell him what I know now—about love and life and loss, about acceptance and forgiveness and peace. This is the hope on the other side of despair, the one we were never sure was coming. *I waited*, I want to tell him. *I waited and it came.*

In my mind he laughs gently at me. He already knows.

———

Mom, Dad, Sister, Matt wrote at the end of his note:

[T]o you I apologize more than anyone. I know you gave everything you had & that you'd willingly have given more. You truly are the most beautiful people in the world to me and, when no one else could cut, you were always the ones to keep me from going to where I am today. Whether it was guilt or love & whether it matters which I do not know, but I am more grateful to you than you could ever imagine or than I could ever show . . .

Sister, the word that stung me all those years ago, the word that felt empty, false, forced, is now tender. Suffused with memory and meaning. Bond. Blood.

I feel him with me all the time. See him in my reflection, hear him in my voice. There is room hollowed out for him in my heart, and a standing invitation, if there is a part of him out there beyond our memories, to join me on what's left my journey.

Please, please forgive me.

I didn't think it would ever be possible, but I do. I do.

surfacing

The neighborhood where we lived in Alabama had a community swimming pool. It was small but clean. An aqua rectangle surrounded by pebbled cement, with a cobwebbed bathroom and a splintered picnic table, a rise of trees on one side of the wrought-iron fence and a slope of grass on the other.

In the summer, my friends and I went swimming there nearly every day. We played a game called Watermelon. It was easy to play: all you had to do was curl up into a ball at the edge of the deep end—knees pulled up under your chin, arms wrapped tightly around your shins, eyes closed—and fall forward into the water. Despite my lack of swimming prowess (and the fact that I had to pinch my nose shut), I liked Watermelon. Tumbling weightlessly in the dark, my ears full of muted rush. My body, the whole world, moving impossibly slowly, my mind silenced by the dizzying sensation.

You were supposed to keep your eyes closed the entire time you were underwater, the delight of the exercise being that you wouldn't know what direction you'd be facing, or how far you'd drifted, until you surfaced. No matter how hard you tried to focus when you rolled in, to picture your surroundings spinning with you, you came up gasping for air and staring at the trees, or the bathroom hut, or the picnic table, or your friend's feet, like you'd never seen them before. It always took a second or two to figure out which direction you were facing. To match the picture you'd imagined, expected, with the one that actually appeared.

■■■■

For the first few years after Matt's death, the cold, colorless stretch between January and April unraveled me, and the end of winter— the melting snow, the breaking ice, the hopeful purple heads of cro- cuses—was my brother, whom I loved, whom I would have done any- thing for, fighting and failing all over again. But in January 2009, the fifth year after his death, I felt . . . good. Better than good—I felt happy. By February, I was downright chipper. Ryan and I spent a week in Costa Rica, and I came home tan, relaxed, completely in love with the Pacific, and ready to face the rest of the winter. I was cau- tiously optimistic. *Is this it?* I thought to myself. *Is it finally happen- ing? Am I finally okay?*

Then March came, and with it a full-body thrum of anxiety that made the fillings in my molars ache. I wanted to squeeze my head into a vise and pop it like a balloon.

Not quite the heavy, hopeless sinking I'd experienced in years past, but by then I'd stopped asking questions. Grief was a greased, rabid animal that could twist itself into any shape, sink its teeth into any part of you. So I settled in, held on, and thanked the good Lord for the shorter stretch.

But the fifth anniversary passed and the restlessness stayed.

In fact, by the end of summer, it had morphed into a full-blown breakdown. I was sick of the city I lived in, the people I knew. I was convinced I was living the wrong life, that I'd been living the wrong life for years—even back before my brother's death. I'd gone to the wrong schools, moved to the wrong city, made the wrong friends. Somewhere, in a parallel universe, the life I was supposed to have was waiting. The person I was supposed to be existed, and she was all the roads I hadn't taken: she'd studied abroad in college and spoke Spanish fluently; she'd just finished her PhD and published her sec- ond book. She lived in a small, sunny house in California, with a long-haired, tattooed poet who read the same books she read and loved the same music she loved. She wasn't married.

Ryan and I went to counseling.

"This makes sense," the counselor said to us. "You got married at a very early age. You didn't get that chance to go out into the world on your own, to establish an independent identity." To me he said, "Almost as soon as you entered the working world, your brother's death took you out of it. Writing this book has been a great way to cope with your grief, but it's left you completely dependent on your husband financially and emotionally. You've isolated yourself."

The counselor went on to talk about my options. I could go back to work, even just part-time. I could take a more active role in the financial management of our daily lives. I could develop stronger relationships outside the marriage, spend more time with friends.

I didn't want to do any of those things. I wanted to wipe the slate clean, start over, be free. Because I couldn't turn back the clock, couldn't relive the last thirty years (or at least the last five), I wanted to break into a life sprint to make up for all the time I'd lost.

"I need to leave," I told Ryan. He took a deep breath, bit his lip.

"Do you need to leave me?"

"I don't think so. . . . Maybe. . . . I don't know."

He ran his hand through his hair, clutched at the back of his neck. "Just . . . just do whatever it is that you need to do."

I started looking for jobs teaching English as a second language. Japan, Spain, Africa. Most programs were two years. That was too long. Could we make it if I left for a year? How about six months? What would happen if I left for six months? Three months. I could go for three months.

But where could I go for three months? And could I really go somewhere for three months alone? I shifted my fantasy to a week-long wilderness excursion, a hike through the Rocky Mountains with nothing but a sleeping bag, a couple jars of peanut butter, and some granola. Then I thought about spiders, bears, long cold nights on hard cold ground. For a while after that I dreamed about Paris. Cafés, museums—a beautiful language that I didn't speak, jet lag, a dearth of vegetarian food.

Besides, would running away solve anything? Or would the restlessness follow me? What would I do then? I was standing at the edge of something, dangerously close to falling in. I was losing my mind, and I was fairly sure that if I didn't figure out what this feeling was, this desperate inside-out scramble, I'd end up just like my brother.

"Tell me what you need," Ryan kept saying. "Whatever you want, we'll make it happen. Just tell me."

I didn't have a fucking clue.

The counselor kept using the word *independence*. It was one of the reasons he suggested I take a trip. Back when the summer was wilting into fall, when the future of my marriage was a giant question mark and every day I scoured the Internet for volunteer opportunities out of state, out of country, out of continent, I said to him, "I need to *go* somewhere. I need to *do something*—by myself."

"I agree," he said. "What's an ideal location for you? What don't you have here that you want?"

It was November in Chicago. Bare branches, cloudy skies, morning frost.

"Sunshine," I said. "Warmer weather, definitely."

"Anything else?"

I remembered the last time I'd been happy—that February, when Ryan and I had gone to Costa Rica. Despite our previous trips to California, it was the first time I'd ever been in the Pacific Ocean. Cold and strong, the waves crashing with thuds loud enough to hear from blocks away. We took a surfing lesson together, and the first time I got up on the board, I bit it big-time—heels over head, dragged under by the current, no clue as to which way was up. It was pure fear, a feeling without words. But after I stood, found my balance, recovered my sense of direction, I realized that I was fine. I got back on my board, paddled out, and rode a wave all the way in, the rush of the ocean beneath me smooth, fast, and fierce—but conquerable. The next time I fell, I let everything go, all sounds muted under the water, my eyes closed, my body spinning, my head empty, until I broke the surface. I imagined later that night that those moments underwater—the world far away, no need for thoughts or language, still myself though consumed by something greater—might be what it's like to be dead. Or waiting to be born.

"Water," I said to the counselor. "I want to be near the ocean."

In December 2009, ten months after the restlessness had started, I boarded a plane to San Francisco for my week of "independence." I'd rented an apartment in wine country for a week, and I planned to isolate myself completely. I wouldn't check my email, wouldn't talk to anyone on the phone—not my parents, not my husband. I thought maybe part of the problem, or at least part of why I couldn't identify the problem, was that I couldn't close myself up tight enough at home. Too much had gotten through, gotten in. I needed to regroup, to seal up the cracks.

I spent days walking around Sonoma, eating olives, and drinking good wine. I went hiking. I read books and watched reruns of *Buffy the Vampire Slayer*. I soaked up afternoon sunshine, wallowed in the scent of eucalyptus and the sound of birds. I tried to write. I stood in the center of my silent, empty rental apartment, neck-deep in a pool of loneliness.

Thousands of miles away from Chicago, from clinking beer bottles, traffic jams, and gray slush, from my husband and my parents and the ghost of my brother, Sonoma was warm, slow, quiet, and calm. Everything I'd wanted. And yet the cracks seemed even larger. I felt even further away from discovering the reason for my restlessness.

———

It wasn't until the day before I left that I got around to driving to the ocean.

Every other shoreline I've visited has leveled off well in advance, sloped down the road to meet the sea. But there the pavement rises like gathered ribbon, up and down over grass hills dotted with sheep and cows. At the crest of every swell I expected the road to drop straight into the water. But it didn't. Maybe this is just how it goes sometimes. The closer you get to your destination, the harder it is to see.

Finally, though, the road cut through a hill, the earth so close I could reach out the window and touch it, and I saw dry stalks of marsh grass. The road curved north, began to twist and turn erratically—and there it was, finally, a glimpse of blue in the distance, saltwater-taffy stands and trailers selling bait and tackle. The road swung to follow the shoreline, and a hundred feet below the biggest waves I have ever seen crashed. The spray was so strong, and so frequent, that a mist hovered over the surface of the water.

I drove for a while before deciding to pull over. All the beaches were accessible only by staircases or steep, sandy embankments. I picked my way down to the water and took off my shoes.

There were other people around, but they were far away. The waves were so loud, the wind so strong, that I couldn't even hear their voices—though I saw their mouths moving. Parents laughed and pointed cameras, children shouted and chased seagulls. I let the very edge of the spent waves wash up over my toes. The water was freezing. I walked back up to the warm, dry hills of sand, lay back, and closed my eyes. *Boom hiss* went the waves, *thump thump* went my heart. The sun burned the back of my eyelids orange. I listened, I breathed. I thought about the water.

I thought about the waves in Costa Rica—the ones I fell into off my surfboard—that made me think of birth and death. The long pause surrounding this living. I thought about being underwater, of spinning weightless, feeling lost, playing Watermelon with my friends in our neighborhood pool.

Grief was like being underwater: everything slow, dark, muted. Grief was like Watermelon. For four and half years, I spun and sank. I lost all sense of direction.

I picked up a rock, worn smooth and warm, and everything was clear: it wasn't Ryan or Chicago. The restlessness had been rooted in grief all along—rooted in its absence. I had spun, sunk, and *risen*. And when I broke the surface, I was miles away from shore. From the life I recognized, the one I expected. The restlessness had been my heart trying to beat hard enough to break down years of walls, my head struggling to recognize my life stripped of the familiar lens of loss. The restlessness had been me searching for my bearings.

In a few hours, after I'd returned to the rented apartment, I would call Ryan and tell him about the ocean, the warmth of the sun, the power of the waves. I'd call my parents and tell them about the gathered ribbon of the road. The next morning I would go hiking, sit on a bench at the top of one of those grass-covered hills, and soak up some silence to take home.

But first I walked back up to the car, knocked the sand out of my sneakers. For miles I drove parallel with west, windows down, hair blowing, sun sinking to the horizon, waves big enough to break a body to bits generating a steady cloud of spray a dozen feet above the water.

There is so much beauty in this violence. From a distance.

epilogue: the whole truth

After I finished my manuscript, I sent it to my parents. I called them to ask what they thought about it. We talked about how difficult it was to turn reality into a story, how hard it was to think about people like characters, how writing about the painful and the personal required detachment and objectivity. I asked my mother, tentatively, if she was okay with its being published, and she paused.

"How important would you say it is to you to know the whole truth?" she asked.

My heart stopped. *The whole truth? What could that possibly mean? What could I be missing? Another letter? One that undoes everything I've discovered? One that tells me I was right all along—it was my fault. One that says not only did I let him down, I destroyed him. One that says he hates me. Curses me. Hopes I burn in hell for everything I've done. One that negates all the words I've written, pisses all over my measure of peace.*

I paused for a moment to consider everything I'd discovered after his death, how it changed him. Changed me. At first I had thought I'd ruined our history, wished I'd never started digging, but after a while I'd realized that the new truth felt even better than the old one. I'd felt closer to him, been grateful to learn that the world outside my head was not always what I'd assumed it to be. I decided that as difficult as it might be to hear, whatever damage it might do, the truth was the whole point of our story. *Okay, then—deep breath.*

"Important. Why?"

"Well, your father and I talked about this. We had decided not to tell you, but the more I thought about it . . . well, I don't want you to get in trouble or anything. I mean, I don't know how many people actually know this, probably just us and I guess the police—"

"Know *what*?"

"Well, you know those nails you wrote about, in that doorway?"

"Yes . . ."

"That's not where he died. He did it in the bathroom, on the shower curtain rod."

I thought about all the years that had passed since the day we'd cleaned out Matt's apartment, all the nights I'd imagined his body suspended in that doorway. The story I'd been writing for myself then, before I'd realized it, and continued writing even after I was supposed to have recognized that I'd been stuck inside my own head, constructing his narrative out of assumptions. I couldn't help it—I started to laugh.

"But I tested it, it was so loose."

"That's because it was broken."

"I'm sorry," I said, still laughing. "I just thought, the way you said that, I thought it was going to be something really bad."

"Well, it seemed like it was an important detail. . . ."

But for once, it wasn't.

Memories fade and surface, questions are asked and answered, points of view shift. My relationship with my brother doesn't stop because he's dead, but his place in my life and in my heart will continue to change. And I suspect that the years to come—births and deaths, people and places, music and poetry—will continue to reach into the past and revise our story.

For better or worse, Matt's life shaped mine. Knowing him, being a sister to him, made me who I was. Losing him has made me who I am.

Yet somewhere on a point beyond the timeline, in spite of everything I've learned, no matter what the future or its effect on the past may bring, I know, I feel, that we are still and will always be just us—a different kind of same.

acknowledgments

Some people say it takes a village. Well, this book took a metropolis.

First off, I'd like to thank StoryStudio Chicago. Had I not discovered this amazing collective, this story would never have found its way out of my head and onto the page. Specific thanks to the SSC memoir crew, especially Annette Gendler, Barbara Coe, Sandy Suminski, Stephanie Springsteen, and Gillian Marchenko. I also want to express the utmost gratitude to the Ragdale Foundation for giving me the time and space to put these pages into some kind of meaningful order. Thanks to Liz Smith, Allison Wolcott, Matt Bourjaily, and Meghan Boyer for first reads, good advice, and support. Thanks to Myron Tuman, Beth Burmester, Lisa Fairman, Sara Hendricksen, and Mary Bowers for second reads, more good advice, and more support. Much appreciation for Brooke Warner, Cait Levin, and She Writes Press for pioneering the next wave in publishing and giving this book a home.

A shout-out to the DDPP Chicago crew for giving me a place of joy during hard times—you ladies made (and continue to make) life worth living. Joe, Jamie, Adam, Jon, Robb, Jared, and Sabrina: thank you for sharing your memories and continuing to stay in touch. Matt loved you deeply, and my family and I love you, too. To all of Matt's other friends: thank you for making him laugh, making him cry, getting him drunk, getting him laid, listening to music with him, talking about politics, and eating shitty food really late at night. Thank you for *living* with him.

No story is the whole story. I regret that there wasn't enough room to show how fiercely awesome my Alabama friends were/are, and how much they did to save my life.

Gratitude and love to my sprawling extended family. You guys have been there in body and spirit, and your hugs and prayers have seen us through.

Finally, most importantly, to my husband and my parents: there are no words for the everyday, one-step-at-a-time love and support you've provided me. You believed in me and trusted me enough to let me to share your lives and your pain on these pages. I thank you from every corner of my heart, and I hope to God I did you some kind of justice.

questions
for discussion

1. What does the author think causes mental illness? Do you agree or disagree? Why?

2. In the chapters "Q & A" and "Telling Stories," the author provides lists of the symptoms of depression and bipolar disorder. Why are mental illnesses so difficult to diagnose? Why are they difficult to treat?

3. How did the author feel about her diagnosis of depression as a teenager? How does she feel about it now? Has the stigma of mental illness changed over the years? Why do you think this stigma exists?

4. Kelley and Matt's upbringing was defined by silence. How common do you think it is for adults to hide life's difficulties, and their own personal struggles, from children? When it comes to family histories of mental illness or addiction, how much is appropriate to share?

5. Art, music, and literature play important roles in the lives of the author and her brother. In the chapter "Music and Lyrics," Kelley recalls how her relationship with writing changed after she began taking medication for depression. Do you think

there is a link between creativity and mental illness? How important do you think creativity is to our sense of well-being?

6. For many years after her brother's suicide, the author felt she was to blame. She eventually came to the conclusion that you can help only those who want to be helped. Do you agree with this? How much influence do you believe we have over the lives of our loved ones?

7. The author struggles with self-imposed expectations when it comes to her grief. Where do these expectations come from? How does she ultimately overcome them?

8. The search for identity is a major theme in this book. Does the author believe that she and her brother's true selves can be separated from their illnesses? Do you agree or disagree?

9. When Kelley and Matt were children, their mother was a devout Catholic. How did Kelley's experience with the church form her understanding of peace? How did that understanding change over the years?

10. What do you think about the title of this book? How are the author and her brother the same? How are they different?

11. What were your thoughts about suicide before reading this book? Have those thoughts changed? If so, what are they now?

resources

There are dozens of organizations in the United States devoted to suicide prevention, support for survivors of suicide, and people living with mental illness. At first Google, the number of hits can be overwhelming. I've narrowed down the list to just a few of the resources I found most helpful during my own period of grieving. You can find more links at my website: www.kelleyclink.com

For Survivors:

The American Foundation for Suicide Prevention
www.afsp.org
The AFSP is a national not-for-profit organization "exclusively dedicated to understanding and preventing suicide through research, education and advocacy, and reaching out to people with mental disorders and those impacted by suicide." The AFSP provides information and support for survivors of suicide, mental health professionals, those living with mental illness, and the general public.

The American Association of Suicidology
www.suicidology.org
The AAS promotes research, public awareness programs, public education, and training for professionals and volunteers. It offers a support-group directory for survivors of suicide, as well as information, support, and a blog for suicide-attempt survivors.

Suicide Prevention Initiatives

www.suicidepreventioninitiatives.org

SPI develops, implements, and funds suicide prevention projects in the United States and worldwide. SPI also provides support to survivors of suicide. In furtherance of these goals, SPI undertakes educational projects aimed at mental health professionals who deal with suicidal patients or survivors, as well as educational and outreach projects intended for the public. Current initiatives include prevention education in China and Vietnam and reducing suicide among veterans.

Suicide Prevention Resource Center

www.sprc.org

SPRC's website offers a comprehensive library/resources section. It also provides a PDF listing key organizations, websites, and materials that provide information and support for survivors of suicide loss (www.sprc.org/sites/sprc.org/files/Survivors.pdf).

For Mental Illness:

Depression and Bipolar Support Alliance

www.dbsalliance.org

DBSA provides a listing of support groups, educational information, and tips on finding professional help, along with a database of clinicians. Its website also features comprehensive wellness and resources sections.

National Alliance on Mental Illness

www.nami.org

NAMI advocates for access to services, treatment, support, and research. It offers an information/help line (1-800-950-NAMI); an education, training, and peer support center; interactive group forums; a veterans/military resource center; a faith network; legal support; and more.

Recommended Reading:

As the stigma attached to suicide and mental illness lessens, the number of books on these subjects increases. These are only a few of the titles I found helpful in the years after Matt's death. Please visit my website for a more comprehensive list.

Night Falls Fast: Understanding Suicide,
by Kay Redfield Jameson

An Unquiet Mind: A Memoir of Moods and Madness,
by Kay Redfield Jameson

The Noonday Demon: An Atlas of Depression,
by Andrew Solomon

Silent Grief: Living in the Wake of Suicide,
by Christopher Lukas

Prozac Diary,
by Lauren Slater

about the author

© M.R. Clink

Kelley Clink is a full-time writer with degrees in literature from the University of Alabama and DePaul University. Her work has appeared in magazines and literary journals including *Under the Sun, South Loop Review, Gettysburg Review, Colorado Review,* and *Shambhala Sun.* She is the winner of the 2014 Beacon Street Prize in Nonfiction. She lives near Chicago with her husband and son.

SELECTED TITLES FROM SHE WRITES PRESS

She Writes Press is an independent publishing company
founded to serve women writers everywhere.
Visit us at www.shewritespress.com.

Breathe: A Memoir of Motherhood, Grief, and Family Conflict by Kelly Kittel
$16.95, 978-1-938314-78-0
A mother's heartbreaking account of losing two sons in the span of nine
months—and learning, despite all the obstacles in her way, to find joy
in life again.

Fire Season: A Memoir by Hollye Dexter
$16.95, 978-1-63152-974-0
After she loses everything in a fire, Hollye Dexter's life spirals downward
and she begins to unravel—but when she finds herself at the brink of
losing her husband, she is forced to dig within herself for the strength to
keep her family together.

Splitting the Difference: A Heart-Shaped Memoir by Tré Miller-Rodríguez
$19.95, 978-1-938314-20-9
When 34-year-old Tré Miller-Rodríguez's husband dies suddenly from
a heart attack, her grief sends her on an unexpected journey that culmi-
nates in a reunion with the biological daughter she gave up at 18.

Green Nails and Other Acts of Rebellion: Life After Loss by Elaine Soloway
$16.95, 978-1-63152-919-1
An honest, often humorous account of the joys and pains of caregiving
for a loved one with a debilitating illness.

Her Beautiful Brain: A Memoir by Ann Hedreen
$16.95, 978-1-938314-92-6
The heartbreaking story of a daughter's experiences as her beauti-
ful, brainy mother begins to lose her mind to an unforgiving disease:
Alzheimer's.

A Leg to Stand On: An Amputee's Walk into Motherhood by Colleen Haggerty
$16.95, 978-1-63152-923-8
Haggerty's candid story of how she overcame the pain of losing a leg at
seventeen—and of terminating two pregnancies as a young woman—
and went on to become a mother, despite her fears.